Unlocking the Power of Heritage Journaling

Your Guide to Writing Personal and Family History

Dovie Archer
PRESS

DovieArcher@gmail.com

Copyright (c) 2024 Dovie Archer

All rights reserved.

Table of Contents

Table of Contents	iii
Welcome and Overview	1
Chapter 1: Understanding Heritage Journaling	5
Chapter 2. Who Should Practice Heritage Journaling and Why?	9
Chapter 3. What Heritage Journaling Brings to Personal and Family History	13
Chapter 4. Starting Your Heritage Journaling Journey	19
Chapter 5: Journaling Through Cultural Signposts	23
Chapter 6: Connecting Across Generations	49
Chapter 7: Embracing Common Traditions	67
Chapter 8: Celebrating Milestones and Everyday Moments	73
Chapter 9: Final Reflections and Encouragement	97
Appendix	1
Inspirational Quotes	2
Affirmations for Writers	10

A family's heritage is the bridge between the past and the future, connecting generations with the wisdom of time.

Welcome and Overview

Welcome, fellow enthusiasts, to the captivating world of Heritage Journaling—a transformative writing practice that breathes life into the names and dates of our family trees. In this journey, we invite you to explore the depths of your ancestry, unlocking stories that go beyond the mere facts and figures of genealogy. Heritage Journaling is not just about tracing your roots; it's about feeling the heartbeat of your history, hearing the whispers of your ancestors, and crafting a living, breathing narrative that binds generations together.

An Introduction to Genealogy and its Evolving Landscape

Genealogy, the art of tracing familial connections through time, has undergone a remarkable evolution. Once confined to dusty archives and yellowing documents, genealogy has now become a dynamic field fueled by technology and a growing curiosity about personal heritage. No longer a pursuit solely for seasoned genealogists, it has opened its doors to novices, drawing in a diverse community eager to unravel the tales hidden in their DNA.

As genealogy has shifted from a mere compilation of names and dates to a vibrant exploration of personal narratives, the landscape has expanded. We are now on a quest not just for information but for the essence of our ancestors' lives—their dreams, struggles, and everyday moments that shaped our familial tapestry. This evolution marks a profound shift from a rigid, academic pursuit to a more holistic and personal exploration of our familial identity.

The Role of Heritage Journaling in the Genealogical Journey

Enter Heritage Journaling—the catalyst that propels genealogy from a static map to a living, breathing landscape. More than just a companion to genealogical research, Heritage Journaling is a practice that enriches the very essence of our familial discoveries. It's an art form that allows us to capture the vibrancy of family stories, preserve the intangible heritage that words alone can convey, and connect us to our roots on a deeper level.

As we delve into the past, Heritage Journaling serves as a guiding light, illuminating the often overlooked facets of our ancestry. It empowers us to move beyond the skeletal framework of family trees, urging us to explore the emotional landscape—the stories of love, resilience, and triumph that shaped our heritage.

This practice encourages a shift from a detached observer to an engaged storyteller, giving life to those who came before us. It transforms genealogy from a passive act of data collection to an active participation in our own ancestral saga. Heritage Journaling is not confined to a linear timeline; it's a dynamic and creative process that invites us to engage with our past, present, and future.

In the pages that follow, we will navigate the realms of unlocking ancestral vaults, exploring cultural catalysts, and preserving the unique heritage that binds us together. With curated prompts, writing exercises, and thoughtful reflections, this journey promises to be both enlightening and deeply enriching.

So, with a heart full of curiosity and a pen poised for exploration, let's embark on this odyssey of Heritage Journaling—a practice that not only transforms how we perceive our ancestry but leaves an indelible mark on the way we connect with our familial roots. Welcome to a journey that transcends time and breathes life into the silent echoes of our heritage.

"To know who you are,

you have to know where

you came from.

Esther Perel

Chapter 1: Understanding Heritage Journaling

In the vast landscape of genealogy, where names and dates often dominate, Heritage Journaling emerges as a powerful tool, transforming the way we perceive, preserve, and celebrate our familial history. This chapter delves into the essence of Heritage Journaling, uncovering its layers, and unraveling the elements that make it a compelling practice for family historians and enthusiasts alike.

Defining Heritage Journaling

At its core, Heritage Journaling is the art of capturing the soul of our ancestry through written reflection. It's more than a record-keeping exercise; it's a narrative journey that transcends the confines of mere facts and figures. In the tapestry of genealogy, Heritage Journaling stitches together the threads of stories, memories, and emotions, creating a vivid tableau of our familial heritage.

This practice is not bound by rigid rules or structured formats. Instead, it encourages a fluid and creative exploration of our roots. Heritage Journaling invites us to be storytellers, weaving narratives that breathe life into the names and dates on our family trees. It's a dialogue with the past, a conversation across generations, where the pen becomes a bridge connecting us to our ancestors.

Unpacking the Elements: Storytelling, Reflection, and Record-Keeping

Heritage Journaling comprises three essential elements—storytelling, reflection, and record-keeping—that harmonize to create a holistic and meaningful exploration of our familial history.

Storytelling is the heartbeat of Heritage Journaling. It's the art of crafting narratives that go beyond the surface of genealogical data. Through storytelling, we transform ancestors from distant figures to living characters with dreams, aspirations, and challenges.

Reflection adds depth to the journey. It's a pause in the rush to uncover names and dates—a moment to ponder, question, and explore the emotional landscape of our heritage. Reflection invites us to consider not just *what* happened but *why* it matters and *how* it shapes our present.

Record-keeping provides the foundation. It ensures that the stories and reflections are preserved for posterity. While traditional genealogy focuses on collecting data, record-keeping in Heritage Journaling involves documenting the emotional nuances and personal narratives that define our familial history.

The Evolution of Genealogy

Genealogy has evolved from a rigid pursuit of lineage to a dynamic exploration of personal narratives. While traditional genealogy primarily concerned itself with constructing family trees and compiling data, the evolution of this field has broadened its scope. Today, genealogy is a vibrant endeavor that seeks to unearth not just names and dates but the stories that give life to those names.

This evolution reflects a societal shift in our approach to history and heritage. As individuals, we are no longer satisfied with the mere accumulation of data; we crave a connection to the human experiences that shaped our past. Heritage Journaling is a response to this shift, offering a more intimate and engaging way to interact with our familial history.

Shifting from Facts to Family Narratives

The traditional approach to genealogy often reduced our ancestors to statistics—a list of birth and death dates, marriages, and locations. While these facts are essential, they only scratch the surface of our familial tapestry. Heritage Journaling encourages a shift from the cold, hard facts to the warm, human stories that breathe life into our family histories.

Through this shift, we move from viewing our ancestors as distant figures to understanding them as individuals who lived, loved, and faced the complexities of their times. We uncover the narratives of resilience, courage, and everyday triumphs that may not be documented in official records but form the heart of our familial heritage.

The Need for a More Holistic Approach

In our quest to understand our roots, a more holistic approach is essential. Heritage Journaling invites us to embrace the complexities of our familial histories—the triumphs and tribulations, the joys and sorrows. It acknowledges that our ancestors were not one-dimensional figures but multifaceted individuals with stories waiting to be told.

This holistic approach extends beyond genealogy as a solitary pursuit. It acknowledges the interconnectedness of families and communities, recognizing that our personal histories are woven into the broader fabric of cultural and historical narratives. Heritage Journaling thus becomes a tool not only for personal self-discovery but for contributing to the collective tapestry of human history.

As we journey further into Heritage Journaling, let us embrace this shift in perspective—from viewing our ancestors as names on a chart to recognizing them as protagonists in the rich narrative of our familial history. Through the art of storytelling, reflection, and record-keeping, we embark on a transformative exploration that goes beyond facts and figures, offering a deeper understanding of who we are and where we come from.

Chapter 2. Who Should Practice Heritage Journaling and Why?

Embarking on a genealogical journey can be an enriching and rewarding experience for individuals from all walks of life. In this chapter, we explore why Heritage Journaling is a practice that resonates with a diverse audience and how it can become a meaningful tool for those at different stages of their genealogical pursuits.

Beginners' Guide: Making Genealogy Accessible for Newcomers

Journaling serves as a welcoming gateway for beginners in genealogy. Explore prompts designed to ease newcomers into the world of family history, providing a structured approach to recording their discoveries, emotions, and aspirations. Your journal becomes a companion on the early steps of your genealogical journey, ensuring that the exploration of your cultural heritage is accessible and enjoyable.

How Heritage Journaling Can Be a Perfect Starting Point

Uncover prompts that guide you through the process of making Heritage Journaling your starting point in genealogy. Reflect on the simplicity and effectiveness of using a journal to record your family history pursuits. Your journal serves as a foundational tool, offering an organized and introspective space to initiate and document your genealogical journey.

For the Seasoned Genealogist: Rediscovering Passion Through a New Lens

Explore prompts tailored for seasoned genealogists, inviting them to rediscover their passion for family history through the lens of Heritage Journaling. Reflect on how journaling can reignite the excitement and curiosity that might fade over time. Your journal becomes a revitalizing force, allowing you to approach familiar stories with fresh perspectives and unveiling new layers in your family narrative.

Viewing Family History with Fresh Eyes

Delve into prompts that encourage you to view your family history with a renewed sense of curiosity and wonder. Reflect on how Heritage Journaling can help you break free from preconceived notions and see familiar stories through fresh eyes. Your journal becomes a tool for continuous discovery, inviting you to uncover hidden gems within your family history.

A Family and Community Affair: Building Connections Through Shared Heritage

Journaling is not just an individual endeavor—it can be a shared experience within families and communities. Explore prompts that foster connections through shared heritage, encouraging family members or community members to engage in coll aborative journaling. Your journal becomes a collective narrative, weaving together the threads of diverse perspectives into a rich tapestry of shared history.

The Collective Power of Heritage Journaling

Reflect on prompts that explore the collective power of Heritage Journaling. Consider how engaging in this practice collectively with others amplifies its impact, fostering a sense of shared history and communal identity. Your journal becomes a testament to the collective efforts of a community, enriching the broader narrative of cultural heritage.

Whether you are a newcomer seeking an accessible entry point into genealogy, a seasoned researcher looking to rekindle passion, or part of a family or community eager to build connections through shared heritage, Heritage Journaling is a versatile and inclusive practice. It welcomes individuals at every stage of their genealogical journey, offering a transformative and accessible approach to exploring and preserving cultural heritage.

"The history of our grandparents is remembered not with rose petals but in the laughter and tears of their children and their children's children."

Julie Andrews

Chapter 3. What Heritage Journaling Brings to Personal and Family History

In the pursuit of understanding personal and family history, Heritage Journaling emerges as a transformative practice that goes beyond the realms of conventional genealogy. This chapter explores the profound impact of Heritage Journaling on preserving intangible heritage, capturing oral traditions, adding depth to family stories, connecting generations, enhancing genealogical research, and ultimately, enriching the tapestry of our family histories.

Preserving Intangible Heritage

While tangible heritage comprises physical artifacts and official records, intangible heritage encompasses the essence of our cultural identity—the stories, traditions, and values passed down through generations. Heritage Journaling becomes a vessel for preserving this intangible heritage, capturing the nuances of familial customs, oral traditions, and the unwritten stories that shape our identity. By documenting these intangible elements, we safeguard them from fading into oblivion, ensuring that the rich tapestry of our cultural heritage remains vibrant and alive.

Capturing Oral Traditions, Rituals, and Everyday Nuances

Heritage Journaling invites us to become custodians of our family's oral traditions, rituals, and the everyday nuances that define our existence. Through the written word, we can capture the cadence of a grandparent's storytelling, the rituals that bind generations, and the subtle details of daily life that often escape the formalities of historical documentation. Journaling becomes a time capsule, preserving the melodies of familial voices, the rhythms of cherished rituals, and the beauty found in the ordinary moments that constitute our shared heritage.

Adding Depth to Family Stories

Conventional genealogy often presents a skeletal framework of our ancestors—names, dates, and locations. Heritage Journaling breathes life into these skeletal structures, adding flesh and dimension to the stories of our forebears. By exploring the motivations, challenges, and triumphs that shaped their lives, we transform genealogical research into a narrative journey. Heritage Journaling uncovers the stories behind the names, making the past relatable and resonant with the present.

Connecting Generations

At the heart of Heritage Journaling is the concept of connecting generations. Through shared narratives, the practice becomes a bridge that spans the generation gap, allowing family members of different ages to engage in a meaningful dialogue. Grandparents can impart wisdom, parents can share their experiences, and younger generations can contribute their perspectives. Heritage Journaling fosters a sense of shared history, reinforcing the bonds that tie families together across time.

Bridging the Generation Gap Through Shared Narratives

In a rapidly changing world, the gulf between generations can sometimes seem vast. Heritage Journaling serves as a tool to bridge this gap by providing a platform for the exchange of stories, insights, and experiences. It becomes a shared space where the wisdom of elders mingles with the fresh perspectives of the younger generation, fostering mutual understanding and creating a continuum of shared narratives.

Passing Down the Torch of Family History

Heritage Journaling is not merely a personal endeavor; it is a collective effort to pass down the torch of family history. As we document our own experiences, we contribute to the ongoing narrative of our family. The journal becomes a precious inheritance, passed from one generation to the next, carrying with it the collective wisdom, traditions, and stories that define us. Through this process, Heritage Journaling becomes an act of legacy-building, ensuring that our family history continues to unfold with richness and depth.

Adding Depth to Genealogical Research

While genealogy traditionally focuses on uncovering names and dates, Heritage Journaling propels us beyond this surface-level exploration. It encourages us to delve into the motivations, cultural contexts, and individual stories that underpin the genealogical data. By considering the "why" behind the facts, we gain a more profound understanding of our ancestors, their choices, and the historical forces that shaped their lives.

Beyond Names and Dates: Exploring Motivations and Cultural Context

The motivations that drive our ancestors, as well as the cultural context in which they lived, are vital components of the genealogical puzzle. Heritage Journaling prompts us to explore these dimensions, adding layers of understanding to our family history. By examining the factors that influenced our ancestors' decisions, we gain insights into the broader historical and cultural landscape that shaped their identities.

Enhancing the Richness of Family History

In essence, Heritage Journaling serves as an alchemical process, transforming the raw data of genealogy into a rich and textured narrative. It elevates family history from a collection of facts to a tapestry woven with the threads of individual stories, cultural heritage, and shared experiences. Through this practice, our family history becomes a living, breathing entity—one that resonates with authenticity, depth, and the timeless echoes of the human experience.

As we embark on the journey of Heritage Journaling, we unlock the potential to preserve intangible heritage, bridge generational divides, and breathe life into the stories that define us. This practice becomes a dynamic force that not only enriches our understanding of personal and family history but also contributes to the ongoing narrative of human heritage. In the chapters that follow, we will delve deeper into the practical aspects of Heritage Journaling, exploring techniques, prompts, and exercises that will empower you to embark on this transformative genealogical journey.

" In every conceivable manner, the family is link to our past and bridge to our future."

Alex Haley

Chapter 4. Starting Your Heritage Journaling Journey

Embarking on the path of Heritage Journaling is a deeply personal and enriching endeavor—one that goes beyond the conventional boundaries of genealogy. This chapter serves as a guide, illuminating the essential steps to kickstart your Heritage Journaling journey. From setting the foundation to selecting the right materials, establishing a routine, understanding the power of prompts, and seamlessly incorporating them into your Heritage Journaling practice, we'll navigate the foundational aspects that lay the groundwork for a meaningful exploration of personal and family history.

Setting the Foundation

Before putting pen to paper, it's crucial to set a solid foundation for your Heritage Journaling journey. Begin by clarifying your intentions and goals. What do you hope to discover or achieve through this practice? Whether it's preserving family stories, connecting with your cultural heritage, or deepening your understanding of ancestors, a clear vision will guide your journaling experience. Consider your values, what aspects of your heritage resonate with you, and the themes you wish to explore.

Selecting the Right Materials and Tools

The choice of materials and tools is a personal decision that can significantly impact your Heritage Journaling experience. Select a journal that resonates with you—consider factors like paper quality, size, and whether you prefer lined or blank pages. Choose pens, pencils, or other writing instruments that feel comfortable in your hand. Some individuals find joy in incorporating artistic elements like sketches, photographs, or mementos. The key is to create a space that inspires creativity and reflection.

Establishing a Regular Journaling Routine

Consistency is the cornerstone of any journaling practice. Establishing a regular routine helps integrate Heritage Journaling into your daily life. Choose a time and space that feels conducive to reflection—whether it's a quiet morning ritual, a peaceful evening sanctuary, or snippets of journaling during the day. Consistent journaling not only ensures a continuous narrative but also serves as a mindful practice, grounding you in the present moment.

The Power of Prompts in Sparking Creativity

Prompts are potent catalysts for unlocking the depths of your Heritage Journaling journey. They provide a gentle nudge when inspiration wanes and guide your reflections in meaningful directions. Explore prompts that resonate with your intentions—whether it's delving into family traditions, exploring cultural nuances, or uncovering hidden stories. The beauty of prompts lies in their ability to ignite creativity, prompting you to see familiar narratives with fresh eyes.

Incorporating Prompts into Heritage Journaling

As you delve into Heritage Journaling, consider prompts as keys that unlock the doors to unexplored realms of your personal and family history. These prompts can take various forms—questions that probe into your cultural background, invitations to recount memorable family gatherings, or reflections on the values passed down through generations. Incorporate prompts organically into your journal entries, letting them guide your reflections while leaving room for spontaneous exploration.

Heritage Journaling, at its core, is a dynamic dance between intention and exploration. It's about fostering a connection with your roots, preserving the intangible threads of cultural heritage, and weaving a narrative tapestry that spans generations. The following sections of this book will delve deeper into the practical aspects of Heritage Journaling, offering a treasure trove of prompts, exercises, and insights to enrich your journey. As you navigate this chapter, remember that your Heritage Journaling journey is uniquely yours, and each entry contributes to a narrative that is both personal and universal.

" It is not the honor that you take with you, but the heritage your leave behind."

Branch Rickey

Chapter 5: Journaling Through Cultural Signposts

Journaling Through Cultural Signposts is a captivating exploration of the rich tapestry that shapes our familial and cultural identity. It's a journey that beckons individuals to decipher the hidden messages embedded in customs, traditions, and the shared experiences of their ancestors. By delving into the significance of cultural signposts, heritage journaling becomes a compass guiding practitioners through the labyrinth of familial narratives.

This theme prompts individuals to unlock the secrets held within ancestral traditions, offering a profound understanding of the customs that have woven the fabric of their family's history. Each journaling entry becomes a step closer to unraveling the stories behind cultural practices, providing a deeper context to one's roots.

Cultural signposts offer a roadmap to heritage, urging journal keepers to document the rituals, ceremonies, and everyday practices that have sustained their families through generations. These prompts encourage reflection on how these cultural signposts have influenced personal beliefs, values, and the collective identity of a family. Through heritage journaling, individuals can celebrate the diversity of their cultural inheritance and create a timeless narrative that pays homage to the enduring significance of these cultural signposts.

Unlocking Ancestral Vaults

Heritage Journaling serves as the key to unlocking the vaults of ancestral stories, hidden in the recesses of time. Begin your journey by contemplating the significance of your family's history. What untold tales lie dormant? Dive into the past, exploring the lives and experiences of those who came before. Use prompts that encourage reflection on family lore, uncovering anecdotes, and understanding the broader context of your ancestors' lives.

Heritage Journaling Prompts

> **The Sealed Letter:** Imagine receiving a sealed letter from an ancestor. Describe the anticipation and excitement as you break the seal. Write down the contents of the letter, exploring the messages, advice, or revelations it contains. Reflect on the significance of this imaginary communication and how it shapes your understanding of that ancestor.
>
> **Ancestral Treasures:** Visualize discovering a hidden room filled with treasures from your family's past. Describe the artifacts, documents, or heirlooms you uncover. Reflect on the historical value and personal significance of these treasures. Consider how these newfound items contribute to your connection with your ancestors.
>
> **Conversations Across Time:** Imagine having a conversation with an ancestor from a different era. Choose a specific ancestor and engage in a dialogue with them. Discuss their experiences, challenges, and triumphs. Reflect on the insights gained from these

imaginary conversations and how they enhance your understanding of your familial roots.

Secrets in the Attic: Explore the metaphorical attic of your family history. Envision finding a dusty box tucked away in a corner, filled with forgotten documents, letters, or photographs. Detail the contents of this box and speculate on the stories behind each item. Reflect on the emotions stirred by uncovering these hidden gems.

The Time-Traveling Photo Album*: Imagine stumbling upon a magical photo album that allows you to travel back in time and witness key moments in your family's history. Choose a significant event and describe the scenes captured in this extraordinary album. Reflect on the impact of visually witnessing pivotal moments in your ancestry.*

Keys to the Past: Envision discovering a set of old keys that open long-forgotten doors within your family's history. Each key corresponds to a different era or aspect of your ancestry. Describe the doors you unlock and the revelations behind them. Reflect on the symbolism of these keys and the newfound understanding they bring.

Roots of Resilience: Consider a challenging moment in your family's history. How did your ancestors navigate adversity? Reflect on the resilience they demonstrated. How can their strength inspire and guide you in facing challenges in your own life?

Family Wisdom Traditions: Explore the traditions and wisdom passed down through generations. What cultural or familial practices have endured the test of time? Reflect on how these traditions contribute to the tapestry of your family's identity and values.

Echoes in Heirlooms: Choose a family heirloom with a story. It could be a piece of jewelry, a photo album, or a handwritten letter. What echoes of the past does this heirloom carry? Reflect on the emotions and memories embedded in these tangible links to your ancestry.

Generational Patterns: Identify recurring patterns or themes within your family tree. It could be a common profession, a shared passion, or even certain challenges. Reflect on how these patterns have influenced the trajectory of your family. Are there aspects you wish to continue or transform?

Ancestral Voices in Nature: Connect with nature in a way that resonates with your ancestry. Visit a place significant to your heritage, or simply spend time outdoors contemplating the elements. What whispers of wisdom do you hear from the natural world that echo the stories of your ancestors?

Celestial Connections: Look to the stars and explore the concept of ancestral constellations. Imagine each ancestor as a star in the night sky. Which constellations would represent different branches of your family? Reflect on the interconnectedness of these celestial representations.

Delving into the Hidden Stories

Every family harbors stories that, over time, may have faded into obscurity. Heritage Journaling offers a space to delve into these hidden narratives. Use prompts that encourage you to interview older family members, seeking out stories that might have been tucked away. Bring these narratives to light, weaving them into your journal entries to create a rich tapestry of familial history.

Heritage Journaling Prompts

Family Lore Unveiling: Journal about a piece of family lore or a mysterious story that has intrigued you. Explore the hidden layers of this narrative, delving into the details, and expressing your curiosity about the truth behind the family tale.

Enigmatic Ancestors: Choose an ancestor with a mysterious past or unclear details. Journal about your quest to unveil the hidden aspects of their life, sharing your thoughts on what might be concealed in the shadows of their history.

Cryptic Letters Analysis: If you have old letters or documents with ambiguous content, transcribe and analyze them. Journal about your efforts to decode the hidden meanings, emotions, or secrets embedded in these written artifacts.

Lost Family Connections: Identify family connections that have been lost or strained over time. Journal about your exploration into reconnecting with estranged relatives, understanding the reasons behind the rifts, and discovering the hidden stories within familial relationships.

Ancestor's Journal Analysis: If you have access to an ancestor's journal or diary, analyze a passage with cryptic or veiled language. Journal about your interpretation of the hidden emotions or events within these writings, speculating on what may be concealed between the lines.

Intriguing Heirlooms: Choose a family heirloom with a mysterious origin or purpose. Journal about your investigation into the hidden stories behind this object, imagining the hands it passed through and the untold tales it carries.

Family Ghosts and Legends: Explore any ghost stories or legends associated with your family. Journal about the hidden cultural beliefs, superstitions, or paranormal tales that have been passed down through generations, expressing your fascination with these mysterious elements.

Unsolved Family Mysteries: Identify an unsolved mystery within your family history. Journal about your commitment to solving this mystery, detailing the steps you'll take to uncover hidden truths and shed light on unresolved aspects of your ancestral past.

Lost Ancestral Homes: If your ancestors had homes or properties that are now lost or unknown, explore the history of these places. Journal about your journey to uncover the hidden stories of these ancestral residences, imagining the lives lived within their walls.

Silent Photographs: Choose a family photograph with unidentified individuals or unclear contexts. Journal about your efforts to unveil the hidden narratives captured in the image, speculating on the stories behind the faces and scenes frozen in time.

Forgotten Achievements: Identify a family member whose achievements or contributions are not widely known. Journal about your determination to highlight and celebrate these hidden accomplishments, ensuring that their legacy is recognized within the family narrative.

Inherited Talents: Reflect on hidden talents or skills that run in your family. Journal about your exploration into uncovering these inherited gifts, expressing your appreciation for the unique abilities that contribute to the richness of your family's story.

Resurrecting Forgotten Narratives

Some stories may have been lost to time, forgotten in the transitions between generations. As you navigate your Heritage Journaling journey, consider prompts that act as a resurrection tool for these forgotten narratives. Explore family photo albums, old letters, or artifacts that may spark memories. By resurrecting these stories, you breathe life into the past and ensure that valuable family legacies are not lost.

Heritage Journaling Prompts

Lost in Time: Reflect on family stories or traditions that have faded into obscurity. Choose one narrative that intrigues you the most and resurrect it through detailed journaling. Explore the fragments of memory and weave them into a vibrant tapestry.

Hidden Gems: Delve into the forgotten corners of your family history. Identify an ancestor or relative whose story remains obscured. Bring this overlooked narrative back to life in your journal, celebrating the uniqueness that may have been buried with time.

The Echo of Ancestral Voices: Capture the echoes of ancestral voices by revisiting old family records, letters, or photographs. Choose a forgotten figure and use journaling to breathe life into their experiences, dreams, and challenges, ensuring their voice reverberates through the generations.

Revisiting Traditions: Explore family traditions that have slipped away with time. Identify one tradition that held significance and has been forgotten. Through detailed journaling, reimagine the steps, sights, and emotions tied to this tradition, reigniting its presence in your family narrative.

The Untold Story: Consider the gaps and silences in your family history. Choose a period or event that remains shrouded in mystery and resurrect the untold story. Use your journal to speculate, imagine, and piece together the narrative that time may have concealed.

Forgotten Journeys: Revisit the journeys of ancestors that time has pushed to the background. Select a forgotten journey, whether it's migration, exploration, or a personal quest. Through journaling, retrace their steps, exploring the challenges, triumphs, and landscapes they encountered.

Relics of the Past: Identify forgotten family artifacts, heirlooms, or objects with untold stories. Select one and use your journal to breathe life into its history. Uncover the tales behind the relic, envisioning the hands that held it and the moments it witnessed.

Legacy in Letters: If you have letters or written records from the past, choose one that hasn't been thoroughly explored. Resurrect the emotions, contexts, and personalities embedded in the words. Your journal becomes a portal to relive the sentiments of bygone correspondences.

Fading Faces: Select old family photographs featuring faces that time may have forgotten. Use your journal to explore the identities, relationships, and stories behind these fading faces. Bring them back into focus through descriptive and reflective writing.

The Abandoned Homestead: Consider ancestral homes or locations significant to your family that have been left behind. Choose one and resurrect its history through journaling. Envision the daily life, gatherings, and memories that echo within its walls.

Ephemeral Traditions: Explore traditions or customs that were once integral but are now fading away. Through your journal, resurrect these ephemeral traditions by documenting their origins, significance, and the role they played in family life.

Whispers of Wisdom: Identify forgotten pieces of wisdom, proverbs, or sayings within your family. Select one and use your journal to explore its origins, meanings, and the circumstances under which it was shared. Resurrect these snippets of ancestral wisdom for contemplation and reflection.

Catalysts for Exploration

Heritage Journaling acts as a catalyst, fueling your exploration of family history in uncharted territories. Utilize prompts that ignite curiosity—questions that prompt you to investigate ancestral connections, explore family migration patterns, or delve into the history of your family's cultural practices. These prompts serve as trail markers, guiding you towards untrodden paths in genealogy.

Heritage Journaling Prompts

The Heirloom Odyssey: Reflect on a significant family heirloom or artifact that has been passed down through generations. Describe its origin, the stories surrounding it, and the emotions it evokes. How does this object connect you to your family's past?

Journey Through Recipes: Explore a cherished family recipe that has been handed down. What culinary delights have been part of your family's history? Write about the occasions, the people involved, and how these recipes have become a thread weaving through generations.

Mapping Memories: Imagine taking a journey to your ancestral homeland. Create a map, marking places significant to your family. Describe the emotions you would feel visiting these locations and the stories you hope to uncover.

Letters Through Time: Write a letter to a past ancestor, expressing your curiosity about their life and asking questions you'd love to have answered. Consider their potential responses and the insights it might provide into your family's narrative.

The Name Chronicle: Dive into the history and meaning behind your family name. Research its origin and any variations over time. How has your surname contributed to your family's identity, and what stories might it hold?

Ancestral Maps: Journal about your intention to create a map of ancestral locations, marking places significant to your family's history. Explore the catalysts that drive your desire to physically explore these places and connect with your roots.

Unexplored Archives: Identify archives or repositories related to your family history that you have yet to explore. Journal about the catalysts motivating you to delve into these untapped resources, envisioning the potential discoveries awaiting you.

Family Migration Routes: Explore the migration routes of your ancestors. Journal about the catalysts prompting you to follow their paths, whether through physical travel or virtual exploration, and the insights you hope to gain from retracing their journeys.

DNA Testing Motivation: If you haven't undergone DNA testing, journal about the catalysts motivating you to do so. Explore your curiosity about genetic connections, ancestral origins, and the potential for discovering unknown relatives.

Untapped Oral Histories: Identify family members with untold stories or oral histories. Journal about the catalysts prompting you to initiate conversations, record interviews, or organize family gatherings to preserve these valuable narratives.

Hidden Family Collections: Explore hidden collections within your family, such as letters, photos, or artifacts stored away. Journal about the catalysts driving you to uncover and catalog these treasures, ensuring they are preserved and shared with future generations.

Heritage Travel Goals: Set heritage travel goals for visiting ancestral locations. Journal about the catalysts motivating you to embark on these journeys, whether to connect with cultural roots, explore family history, or experience the landscapes integral to your ancestry.

Igniting Curiosity in Family History

Curiosity is the compass that guides fruitful exploration. As you embark on your Heritage Journaling journey, stoke the flames of curiosity through thought-provoking prompts. Pose questions that challenge assumptions and encourage you to dig deeper. By fostering a mindset of perpetual inquiry, you'll uncover layers of family history that may have remained concealed.

Heritage Journaling Prompts

Curiosity Catalyst: Reflect on a family mystery or unanswered question that has sparked your curiosity. Journal about your burning desire to uncover the truth, outlining what you hope to discover and how it might reshape your understanding of your family history.

Time-Traveler's Dilemma: Imagine you have the ability to travel back in time and meet one of your ancestors. Journal about the questions you would ask, the experiences you'd want to witness, and the insights you hope to gain. Use this exercise to fuel your curiosity and ignite a deeper connection.

The Enigmatic Photo: Choose a family photo that has always intrigued you. Explore the details, expressions, and background. Journal about the questions it raises and the stories it might hold. Let your curiosity guide you as you contemplate the narratives behind the faces frozen in time.

Letters from the Past: If you have family letters or correspondence, select one that piques your interest. Journal about the emotions, contexts, and relationships embedded in the words. Allow your curiosity to lead the way as you unravel the layers of the past through written exchanges.

Archives Adventure: Plan a visit to a local archive, library, or historical society with the intention of exploring your family's history. Journal about your expectations, the treasures you hope to uncover, and the potential surprises awaiting you in the archives.

Uncharted Branches: Identify a branch of your family tree that you know little about. Journal about your curiosity regarding this particular lineage—what gaps do you want to fill, and how might the exploration of this branch enrich your overall understanding of your family history?

Artifact Detective: Delve into your family's artifacts, heirlooms, or objects with unknown origins. Choose one and journal about your curiosity regarding its history, purpose, and the stories it might hold. Use your imagination to explore the significance behind the artifact.

Intriguing Anecdotes: Recall family anecdotes or stories that have sparked your curiosity. Journal about these tales, expressing your desire to dig deeper, verify details, and understand the motivations behind the narratives. Let your curiosity be the guiding force in uncovering the truth.

Fabled Folklore: Explore family folklore or legends that have been passed down through generations. Journal about your curiosity regarding the origins of these stories—what truths might be hidden within the tales, and how might they connect to real events or individuals?

Curious Connections: Identify unexpected connections or relationships within your family tree. Journal about the surprises or mysteries that arise from these connections, fueling your curiosity to explore the circumstances that led to these unique family ties.

Geographical Quest: Choose a location significant to your family history that you've always been curious about. Journal about your interest in exploring the geography, local history, and cultural context of that place, imagining the lives of your ancestors within that setting.

Interview Inquiry: If there are living relatives with firsthand knowledge of family history, plan an interview. Journal about the questions you want to ask, the insights you hope to gain, and the role curiosity plays in preserving and passing down the family narrative.

Pursuing Untrodden Paths in Genealogy

Traditional genealogy often follows well-worn paths, focusing on names, dates, and familial connections. Heritage Journaling invites you to pursue untrodden paths, seeking the nuances and intricacies that add depth to your family history. Use prompts that encourage you to investigate unconventional aspects—family traditions, cultural influences, or the impact of historical events on your ancestors' lives.

Heritage Journaling Prompts

Exploration Ethos: Journal about your motivation to tread unexplored paths in your genealogical journey. Reflect on the excitement and challenges of venturing into unknown territories, both figuratively and literally, in pursuit of your family's history.

Map of Mysteries: Create a metaphorical map of your family tree, highlighting areas that remain uncharted or mysteries that await unraveling. Journal about your strategy for pursuing these untrodden paths and the anticipation that comes with exploring the unknown.

Hidden Archives Quest: Identify lesser-known archives or repositories related to your family history. Journal about your plans to visit these hidden gems, the anticipation of discovering unique records, and the potential revelations that might emerge from these untapped resources.

Genealogical Archaeology: Imagine yourself as a genealogical archaeologist. Journal about your commitment to digging beneath the surface, uncovering buried stories, and bringing to light the forgotten narratives that lie hidden within the layers of your family's past.

Untold Stories Challenge: Select a branch of your family tree that has received less attention. Journal about the challenges and rewards of delving into this unexplored territory, expressing your commitment to giving voice to the stories that have remained untold.

Ancestor's Footsteps: Choose a location significant to your ancestors that you've never visited. Journal about your plans to follow in their footsteps, exploring the landscapes they once knew. Reflect on the potential insights and connections that might arise from physically traversing untrodden paths.

Legacy of the Unknown: Reflect on the gaps and uncertainties in your family history. Journal about your dedication to filling these voids, the strategies you'll employ, and the potential impact of uncovering the unknown aspects of your ancestral legacy.

Photographic Exploration: Identify old family photos with unidentified individuals or unclear contexts. Journal about your commitment to exploring these visual untrodden paths, using clues and research to unravel the stories captured in these enigmatic images.

Collaborative Discovery: Reach out to distant relatives or fellow genealogists who may hold pieces of the puzzle you seek. Journal about the collaborative effort required to navigate untrodden paths together, sharing insights, and collectively unveiling hidden family history gems.

Cultural Crossroads: Investigate the cultural intersections within your family history. Journal about the unexplored cultural nuances, traditions, or migrations that have shaped your family's identity. Express your curiosity in understanding how these untrodden paths contribute to your ancestral tapestry.

Timeline Resurgence: Revisit your family timeline and identify gaps or periods that lack detailed exploration. Journal about your commitment to resurrecting these forgotten timelines, filling in the missing pieces, and understanding the untrodden paths that shaped your ancestors' lives.

The Journey's Unwritten Chapters: Envision your genealogical journey as a book with unwritten chapters. Journal about your excitement and determination to pen the untrodden paths, documenting the stories that have eluded recognition and ensuring that every aspect of your family's history finds its place in the narrative.

Preserving Cultural Heritage

Preservation is at the heart of Heritage Journaling. Engage with prompts that guide you in documenting traditions and customs passed down through generations. Consider how cultural heritage has shaped your family's identity and values. Use your journal as a repository, safeguarding the richness of your cultural heritage for future generations.

Heritage Journaling Prompts

Cultural Traditions Preservation: Journal about your commitment to preserving cultural traditions within your family. Explore the catalysts driving you to document and pass down rituals, celebrations, and customs that contribute to your cultural heritage.

Language Revitalization: If your family speaks a language at risk of fading away, journal about the catalysts motivating you to revitalize and preserve that language within your family, ensuring its continuity across generations.

Culinary Heritage Cookbook: Commit to creating a cookbook that captures the culinary heritage of your family. Journal about the catalysts behind this project, including preserving traditional recipes, connecting through food, and celebrating the flavors of your cultural background.

Customs Documentation Project: Initiate a project to document unique customs or practices within your family. Journal about the catalysts driving you to compile this cultural anthology, recognizing the importance of preserving customs that may otherwise be lost with time.

Festivals and Celebrations Archive: Create an archive dedicated to family festivals and celebrations. Journal about the catalysts motivating you to document these events, capturing the essence of cultural festivities and fostering a sense of identity within your family.

Cultural Artifacts Catalog: If your family possesses cultural artifacts, create a catalog of these items. Journal about the catalysts behind preserving these tangible elements of your heritage, recognizing their significance in conveying cultural stories.

Music and Dance Preservation: Explore the preservation of traditional music and dance within your family. Journal about the catalysts driving you to document, teach, or perform these artistic expressions, ensuring they endure as living aspects of your cultural heritage.

Historical Family Legends: Identify family legends or historical tales that contribute to your cultural heritage. Journal about the catalysts motivating you to research, document, and share these stories, recognizing their role in shaping your family's cultural identity.

Cultural Clothing Exhibition: Curate an exhibition of cultural clothing within your family. Journal about the catalysts behind preserving and showcasing these garments, understanding the cultural symbolism and significance woven into each piece.

Artistic Heritage Gallery: Create a gallery featuring artwork or crafts passed down through generations. Journal about the catalysts driving you to preserve and display these creations, recognizing their artistic and cultural value within your family.

Heritage Language Learning Project: Initiate a project to learn or teach a heritage language within your family. Journal about the catalysts motivating you to engage in linguistic preservation, fostering communication in a language integral to your cultural roots.

Cultural Heritage Education Initiative: Commit to educating younger generations about their cultural heritage. Journal about the catalysts driving you to create educational materials, workshops, or experiences that impart the importance of cultural preservation to the next family members.

Documenting Traditions and Customs

Your journal becomes a sacred space for documenting the tapestry of traditions and customs that define your cultural heritage. Use prompts to explore the rituals embedded in your family's history. Capture the essence of celebrations, ceremonies, and everyday practices. By documenting these traditions, you contribute to the ongoing narrative of your family's cultural legacy.

Heritage Journaling Prompts

Generational Traditions: Journal about the traditions passed down through multiple generations within your family. Explore the unique customs or rituals that have endured, reflecting on the catalysts that sustain these connections across time.

Seasonal Celebrations: Document the traditions associated with specific seasons or holidays within your family. Journal about the customs, rituals, and familial connections that define these celebratory moments, recognizing their role in shaping your family's cultural identity.

Life Milestone Rituals: Explore the customs related to significant life milestones within your family. Journal about the traditions associated with births, marriages, or other pivotal moments, recognizing the cultural threads that weave through these important occasions.

Ancestral Commemorations: Identify customs or ceremonies dedicated to commemorating ancestors within your family. Journal about the rituals, practices, or annual events that pay homage to those who came before, fostering a connection to ancestral roots.

Daily Routines and Customs: Document the daily routines and customs unique to your family. Journal about the simple, everyday practices that carry cultural significance, recognizing how these small rituals contribute to the larger tapestry of your family's heritage.

Religious Observances: Explore the religious customs observed within your family. Journal about the rituals, ceremonies, or traditions associated with your family's faith, recognizing the cultural and spiritual dimensions intertwined in these practices.

Folklore and Storytelling Nights: Initiate a tradition of storytelling nights within your family. Journal about the catalysts driving you to preserve and pass down folklore, myths, and family stories through these communal storytelling sessions.

Handcrafted Customs: Identify customs or traditions that involve handcrafted elements within your family. Journal about the artistic and cultural significance of these handcrafted items, recognizing their role in preserving and expressing your family's heritage.

Community Celebrations: Explore traditions tied to community celebrations or festivals within your family. Journal about the customs that connect your family to a broader cultural or regional identity, fostering a sense of belonging to a larger community.

Traditional Clothing Rituals: Document the rituals associated with traditional clothing within your family. Journal about the customs related to donning specific attire for special occasions, recognizing the cultural symbolism and storytelling woven into each garment.

Language Preservation Activities: Engage in activities that contribute to the preservation of your family's language traditions. Journal about the rituals or practices involved in language learning, recognizing the importance of linguistic heritage in shaping family culture.

Culinary Customs Exploration: Explore the culinary customs within your family. Journal about the recipes, cooking techniques, or mealtime rituals that carry cultural significance, recognizing the role of food in preserving and sharing your family's unique heritage.

Securing the Legacy of Cultural Practices

Heritage Journaling acts as a custodian, securing the legacy of cultural practices for generations to come. Reflect on prompts that encourage you to contemplate the enduring impact of cultural practices within your family. How have these practices evolved? What do they signify? By securing these legacies in your journal, you ensure that the thread of cultural heritage remains unbroken.

Heritage Journaling Prompts

Interactive Family Cookbook: Create an interactive family cookbook that not only compiles recipes but also includes the stories, rituals, and cultural anecdotes tied to each dish. Journal about the process of securing this culinary legacy for future generations.

Cultural Artifacts Exhibition: Curate an exhibition of cultural artifacts within your family. Journal about the process of selecting, preserving, and showcasing these items, ensuring their cultural significance is understood and appreciated by the next generation.

Family Traditions Handbook: Develop a handbook documenting family traditions. Journal about the creation of this comprehensive guide, including the customs, rituals, and stories that define your family's cultural practices, serving as a roadmap for future generations.

Digital Archive Project: Initiate a digital archive project to preserve cultural practices through multimedia. Journal about your efforts to collect and digitize photos, videos, and audio recordings that capture the essence of family traditions, ensuring a lasting legacy in the digital era.

Generational Storytelling Circle: Establish a tradition of storytelling circles within your family, where each generation contributes narratives and cultural insights. Journal about the collaborative process of securing these stories, creating an interwoven tapestry of cultural practices across generations.

Heirloom Documentation Project: Document the stories and significance behind family heirlooms. Journal about the process of creating a catalog or digital repository that secures the legacy of these artifacts, preserving their cultural and historical value for future family members.

Interactive Ancestral Map: Design an interactive ancestral map that not only marks geographical locations but also includes narratives, rituals, and customs associated with each place. Journal about the creative process of mapping your family's cultural journey.

Virtual Family Museum: Develop a virtual family museum to showcase cultural practices. Journal about the creation of this online space, exploring how it captures the essence of family traditions and serves as a dynamic repository for future generations to explore.

Customs and Traditions Journal: Start a dedicated journal focused on documenting customs and traditions within your family. Journal about the entries, reflections, and the evolving nature of this record as new practices emerge and old ones transform over time.

Storytelling Through Art: Express cultural practices through artistic endeavors. Journal about your exploration of painting, sculpture, or other art forms that convey the essence of family traditions, serving as visual narratives for future generations.

Interactive Family Calendar: Create an interactive family calendar that not only marks important dates but also highlights cultural celebrations and practices. Journal about the collaborative effort to curate and update this living document, ensuring its relevance across generations.

Documentary Project: Undertake a documentary project to capture the living cultural practices within your family. Journal about the process of planning, filming, and editing, recognizing the power of visual storytelling in preserving and sharing your family's unique heritage.

As you navigate the cultural signposts within your Heritage Journaling journey, remember that each entry is a step towards preserving, understanding, and celebrating the vibrant tapestry of your family's history. The following sections of this book will continue to guide you through thematic prompts, exercises, and discussions that enrich your exploration of personal and familial heritage.

Chapter 6: Connecting Across Generations

Connecting Across Generations is a heartfelt odyssey through the intricate threads that weave together family narratives, creating a tapestry of shared identity and understanding. It beckons individuals to traverse the generational landscape, exploring the stories, traditions, and experiences that echo through time.

This theme serves as a compass for heritage journaling practitioners, guiding them to decipher the hidden messages within familial customs and traditions. Much like cultural signposts, the prompts encourage a deep dive into the significance of shared experiences, unraveling the secrets and wisdom that have shaped family histories.

Connecting Across Generations prompts individuals to unlock the treasure trove of stories embedded in ancestral practices. Through heritage journaling, each entry becomes a poignant step towards understanding the rituals that have defined their family's journey. It is an intimate exploration, providing context to one's roots and fostering a profound connection to the past.

These prompts act as a roadmap to heritage, urging journal keepers to document the rituals and ceremonies that have stood the test of time. By reflecting on these cultural signposts, practitioners gain insight into how these practices have influenced personal beliefs and values, contributing to the rich tapestry of a family's collective identity. Heritage journaling, through Connecting Across Generations, becomes a celebration of cultural diversity and a timeless narrative paying homage to the enduring significance of these familial signposts.

A Shared Identity

Heritage Journaling provides a bridge across generations, fostering a shared identity that spans the tapestry of your family's history. Dive into prompts that encourage exploration of the elements that define your family's collective identity. What values, beliefs, or experiences serve as the common threads weaving through generations? Use your journal to articulate and celebrate this shared identity, creating a narrative that resonates across familial epochs.

Heritage Journaling Prompts

Family Crest Exploration: Journal about your family's crest or symbols that represent your shared identity. Reflect on the elements that make up this emblem and explore the stories and values it encapsulates.

Origin Story Unveiling: Dive into the origins of your family's surname or name. Journal about the discoveries, surprises, or historical insights that contribute to shaping your family's shared identity.

Roots Journey Mapping: Create a map tracing the geographical roots of your family. Journal about the places significant to your shared identity and the emotional connections these locations hold for your family.

Coat of Arms Interpretation: Explore the meaning behind your family's coat of arms. Journal about the colors, animals, or symbols used and how they align with the shared identity and values of your family lineage.

Shared Ancestral Talents: Reflect on and journal about any shared talents or skills that have been passed down through generations within your family. Explore how these talents contribute to your shared identity.

Family Motto Reflection: If your family has a motto, explore its origins and meaning. Journal about how this motto encapsulates the principles and beliefs that form the foundation of your shared identity.

Cultural Heritage Showcase: Dedicate a journal entry to showcasing elements of your family's cultural heritage. Explore traditions, customs, or artifacts that contribute to your shared identity, fostering a sense of pride and connection.

Historical Family Achievements: Reflect on and journal about notable achievements or milestones in your family's history. Explore how these accomplishments contribute to your shared identity and the values they represent.

Ancestral Stories Collage: Create a visual or written collage of ancestral stories. Journal about the diverse narratives that contribute to your family's shared identity, fostering a deeper understanding of your roots.

Emblem of Unity: If your family has a symbol or emblem that represents unity, journal about its significance. Reflect on how this emblem fosters a sense of togetherness and shared identity among family members.

Historical Family Resilience: Explore instances of resilience and strength within your family's history. Journal about how overcoming challenges has shaped your shared identity, fostering a sense of fortitude.

Intergenerational Values Tree: Create a metaphorical tree depicting the values passed down through generations. Journal about the roots (ancestors), trunk (shared values), and branches (individual family members) that contribute to your shared identity.

Fostering a Sense of Belonging

A sense of belonging is a powerful force that unites family members across time and space. Through Heritage Journaling, prompts can be crafted to delve into the emotional resonance of family belonging. Explore how shared narratives, anecdotes, or cultural practices contribute to a profound sense of connection. This exploration not only strengthens familial bonds but also nurtures a shared understanding of what it means to belong to a particular family lineage.

Heritage Journaling Prompts

Family Traditions Revisited: Reflect on and journal about cherished family traditions. Explore how these rituals foster a sense of belonging and connection among family members.

Generational Gathering Memories: Journal about memories from generational gatherings. Reflect on how these shared experiences contribute to a sense of belonging and unity within your family.

Shared Accomplishments Celebration: Celebrate and journal about collective accomplishments within your family. Explore how these shared triumphs contribute to a sense of belonging and pride among family members.

Ancestral Pilgrimage: If possible, embark on a journey to ancestral lands. Journal about the emotions, connections, and experiences that foster a profound sense of belonging to your family's roots.

Homeplace Exploration: Explore the history of your family's homeplace. Journal about the significance of this location and how it contributes to a sense of belonging and continuity within your family.

Multigenerational Wisdom Sharing: Reflect on and journal about the wisdom shared across generations within your family. Explore how these shared insights contribute to a sense of belonging and guidance.

Symbolic Family Crest: Create a symbolic family crest that represents your shared sense of belonging. Journal about the elements chosen and how they encapsulate the unity and connection within your family.

Cultural Heritage Potluck: Host a cultural heritage potluck gathering. Journal about the diverse dishes, stories, and traditions shared during this event, fostering a sense of belonging through cultural exchange.

Familial Talents Appreciation: Journal about the unique talents and skills of family members. Reflect on how appreciating and celebrating these individual strengths fosters a collective sense of belonging.

Shared Values Declaration: Create a list of shared values within your family. Journal about the process of identifying and declaring these values, fostering a sense of belonging based on common principles.

Collaborative Family Projects: Engage in a collaborative family project. Journal about the process, challenges, and achievements, reflecting on how working together fosters a deeper sense of belonging.

Interconnected Roots Artwork: Create artwork depicting interconnected roots symbolizing familial connections. Journal about the emotions and reflections that arise during the creative process, fostering a sense of belonging.

Encouraging Dialogue Between Generations

Dialogue is the lifeblood of intergenerational connection. Heritage Journaling prompts can serve as catalysts for meaningful conversations between family members of different ages. Design prompts that encourage the sharing of stories, experiences, and perspectives. By fostering open and genuine dialogue, you create a platform for mutual understanding and appreciation, transcending generational divides.

Heritage Journaling Prompts

Generational Interview Series: Initiate an interview series with family members from different generations. Journal about the insights gained, fostering open dialogue and understanding between the diverse age groups.

Story Circle Gathering: Host a story circle gathering where family members share narratives. Journal about the stories exchanged and the impact of this open dialogue on strengthening connections between generations.

Ancestral Q&A Session: Facilitate a Q&A session where younger family members can ask questions to older generations. Journal about the revelations, shared wisdom, and the bond strengthened through this exchange.

Memory Lane Exploration: Explore a family photo album or memorabilia with members from various generations. Journal about the stories, laughter, and shared memories that surface, fostering a sense of connection.

Shared Hobbies Workshop: Organize a workshop where different generations can share their hobbies or skills. Journal about the diverse talents and the mutual understanding cultivated through this exchange.

Ancestral Recipe Exchange: Initiate a recipe exchange between generations. Journal about the culinary traditions shared, the memories attached to specific dishes, and the intergenerational dialogue facilitated by this activity.

Generational Perspectives Forum: Host a forum where family members from different generations discuss their perspectives on specific topics. Journal about the insights gained, encouraging a respectful and open exchange of ideas.

Historical Technology Session: Create a session where younger generations share modern technology with older family members, and vice versa. Journal about the bridging of technological gaps and the exchange of knowledge between generations.

Generational Book Club: Start a family book club that includes literature reflecting the experiences of different generations. Journal about the discussions, reflections, and insights gained through this shared reading experience.

Life Lessons Letter Exchange: Encourage the exchange of letters between generations, sharing life lessons, experiences, and advice. Journal about the impact of these heartfelt letters on fostering understanding and connection.

Cultural Heritage Documentary Night: Host a documentary night featuring films related to your family's cultural heritage. Journal about the discussions sparked, the shared emotions, and the deepening of connections between generations.

Generational Art Collaboration: Collaborate on an art project that involves members from different generations. Journal about the creative process, insights gained, and the bond strengthened through the shared expression of artistic talents.

A Foundation of Stability

Within the ebb and flow of life, a foundation of stability rooted in shared history provides an anchor for individuals and families. Use Heritage Journaling prompts to explore how family narratives contribute to this foundation. What stories embody stability, resilience, and continuity? Reflect on the ways in which your family's historical experiences serve as a bedrock, offering stability through the passage of time.

Heritage Journaling Prompts

Ancestral Homestead Reflection: Reflect on and journal about your ancestral homestead. Explore the stability it provided for past generations and how it serves as a foundation for family history.

Family Value System Exploration: Explore and journal about the foundational values that have been passed down through generations in your family. Reflect on how these values contribute to stability and continuity.

Shared Family Challenges Journal: Journal about shared challenges that your family has overcome. Reflect on how facing adversity together has contributed to the resilience and stability of your family unit.

Stability Through Family Traditions: Explore the stability provided by family traditions. Journal about the comfort, continuity, and sense of belonging fostered by the consistent practice of these traditions.

Roots and Stability Metaphor: Use a tree roots metaphor to reflect on the stability provided by your family's roots. Journal about how these roots anchor and nourish the family, providing stability in changing times.

Generational Stability Map: Create a map depicting the stability provided by different generations. Journal about the contributions of each generation to the stability and growth of the family unit.

Stability Through Family Residences: Explore the history of family residences and how they symbolize stability. Journal about the memories, milestones, and shared experiences tied to each home, contributing to the family's foundation.

Generational Financial Practices: Reflect on the financial practices passed down through generations. Journal about how these practices contribute to financial stability and resilience within the family.

Family Heirloom Stability: Journal about family heirlooms that represent stability. Explore the stories behind these heirlooms and how they symbolize continuity and a stable connection to the past.

Shared Family Traditions Journal: Reflect on and journal about the shared family traditions that provide stability. Explore how the repetition of these traditions fosters a sense of security and continuity for family members.

Generational Support System: Explore the role of the family as a support system across generations. Journal about how the support provided by family members contributes to the stability of each individual and the family as a whole.

Stability Through Language and Culture: Explore the stability provided by the preservation of language and culture within your family. Journal about the traditions, stories, and rituals that contribute to the cultural stability of your family unit.

Creating Stability Through Shared History

Prompts in this section can guide you in reflecting on specific moments or traditions that have contributed to the creation of stability within your family. Investigate stories of resilience during challenging times, recount instances of collective strength, and explore the stability found in everyday rituals. Your journal becomes a canvas for illustrating the ways in which shared history lays the groundwork for familial stability.

Heritage Journaling Prompts

Generational Timeline Exploration: Create a timeline showcasing significant events in your family's shared history. Journal about the impact of these events on shaping the family's identity and creating stability.

Historical Family Achievements Reflection: Reflect on and journal about historical achievements within your family. Explore how these accomplishments contribute to a sense of pride, stability, and continuity.

Generational Milestones Celebration: Journal about the celebration of generational milestones. Reflect on how marking these milestones contributes to creating stability and a sense of shared history within the family.

Historical Family Challenges Journal: Journal about shared challenges that your family has overcome. Reflect on how facing adversity together has contributed to the resilience and stability of your family unit.

Roots and Stability Metaphor: Use a tree roots metaphor to reflect on the stability provided by your family's roots. Journal about how these roots anchor and nourish the family, providing stability in changing times.

Generational Stability Map: Create a map depicting the stability provided by different generations. Journal about the contributions of each generation to the stability and growth of the family unit.

Stability Through Family Residences: Explore the history of family residences and how they symbolize stability. Journal about the memories, milestones, and shared experiences tied to each home, contributing to the family's foundation.

Generational Financial Practices: Reflect on the financial practices passed down through generations. Journal about how these practices contribute to financial stability and resilience within the family.

Family Heirloom Stability: Journal about family heirlooms that represent stability. Explore the stories behind these heirlooms and how they symbolize continuity and a stable connection to the past.

Shared Family Traditions Journal: Reflect on and journal about the shared family traditions that provide stability. Explore how the repetition of these traditions fosters a sense of security and continuity for family members.

Generational Support System: Explore the role of the family as a support system across generations. Journal about how the support provided by family members contributes to the stability of each individual and the family as a whole.

Stability Through Language and Culture: Explore the stability provided by the preservation of language and culture within your family. Journal about the traditions, stories, and rituals that contribute to the cultural stability of your family unit.

Nurturing Family Bonds Through Heritage

Heritage Journaling is a nurturing space for family bonds to flourish. Design prompts that delve into the emotional landscape of familial relationships. Explore stories that highlight moments of support, camaraderie, or shared achievements. By nurturing an awareness of the emotional fabric woven through generations, you cultivate a deeper understanding of the interconnectedness that defines family bonds.

Heritage Journaling Prompts

Heritage Movie Night: Host a movie night featuring films related to your family's heritage. Journal about the emotions, discussions, and shared experiences that strengthen family bonds.

Cultural Heritage Potluck: Organize a potluck where each family member brings a dish representing their cultural heritage. Journal about the flavors, stories, and connections shared during this culinary exploration.

Generational Stories Exchange: Facilitate an exchange of stories between generations. Journal about the laughter, memories, and bonding moments that arise during this sharing of family narratives.

Ancestral Wisdom Sharing: Reflect on and journal about the wisdom passed down through generations. Explore how sharing ancestral wisdom contributes to the nurturing of family bonds.

Heritage Crafts Workshop: Host a workshop where family members engage in heritage crafts. Journal about the creativity, collaboration, and bonding moments fostered by the shared crafting experience.

Cultural Heritage Trip: Plan a trip to a location significant to your family's cultural heritage. Journal about the discoveries, connections, and shared experiences that strengthen family bonds during the journey.

Generational Photo Recreation: Recreate photos from different generations within your family. Journal about the fun, nostalgia, and bonding moments captured during the process of recreating these memorable images.

Heritage Games Night: Organize a games night featuring traditional games from your family's heritage. Journal about the competitiveness, laughter, and family bonding moments that unfold during the games.

Ancestral Recipe Collaboration: Collaborate on creating a recipe that combines elements from different ancestral backgrounds. Journal about the culinary exploration, teamwork, and family bonding fostered by this collaborative cooking experience.

Multigenerational Art Exhibition: Host an art exhibition showcasing the diverse talents within your family. Journal about the pride, support, and sense of unity generated by appreciating and celebrating each other's artistic expressions.

Heritage Music Jam Session: Arrange a music jam session featuring traditional songs from your family's heritage. Journal about the joy, connection, and shared musical moments that enhance family bonds.

Cultural Heritage Memory Lane: Take a virtual or physical journey through a family memory lane related to cultural heritage. Journal about the stories, emotions, and strengthened bonds as family members reminisce about the past.

A Shared Language of Rituals

Rituals serve as a language that binds generations, creating a shared lexicon that resonates through time. Heritage Journaling prompts can guide you in exploring these rituals, both significant and mundane. Document family traditions, ceremonies, and daily routines that have transcended generations. Celebrate the continuity of these rituals, recognizing the role they play in fostering a shared language that unites family members.

Heritage Journaling Prompts

Generational Ritual Reflection: Reflect on and journal about generational rituals within your family. Explore how these shared practices contribute to a sense of continuity and a shared language among family members.

Cultural Heritage Ritual Showcase: Dedicate a journal entry to showcasing rituals from your family's cultural heritage. Journal about the significance, stories, and shared language embedded in these cultural practices.

Generational Recipe Rituals: Explore and journal about the rituals involved in preparing family recipes passed down through generations. Reflect on the importance of these culinary traditions as a shared language.

Ancestral Celebration Journal: Journal about celebrations that have been passed down through generations. Explore how these shared moments of joy and festivity contribute to a shared language among family members.

Multigenerational Memory Lane: Create a memory lane capturing various generations' experiences of shared rituals. Journal about the emotions, stories, and the evolution of rituals as a shared language.

Family Language Evolution: Reflect on and journal about how the language within your family has evolved over generations. Explore the impact of shared phrases, jokes, and expressions that contribute to a unique family language.

Generational Traditions Collage: Create a visual or written collage depicting generational traditions. Journal about the interconnectedness, stories, and the shared language represented by these traditions.

Cultural Heritage Symbolism: Explore the symbolism embedded in your family's cultural heritage. Journal about the meanings behind specific symbols and how they contribute to a shared language within your family.

Generational Storytelling Circle: Host a storytelling circle where family members share narratives about specific rituals. Journal about the insights, emotions, and the reinforcement of a shared language through these storytelling sessions.

Heritage Language Learning Session: Engage in a language-learning session related to your family's heritage. Journal about the challenges, discoveries, and shared language development experienced during this educational journey.

Generational Traditions Timeline: Create a timeline showcasing the evolution of traditions through different generations. Journal about the changes, adaptations, and the enduring thread of a shared language within these traditions.

Shared Language Artwork: Create artwork representing the shared language of rituals within your family. Journal about the creative process, emotions, and the visual representation of the unique language conveyed through rituals.

Chapter 7: Embracing Common Traditions

Embracing Common Traditions invites explorers of heritage journaling to embark on a profound exploration of the timeless rituals and customs that weave the familial tapestry. This theme serves as a compass, guiding practitioners through the labyrinth of shared practices that define family life. Journal keepers are prompted to uncover the hidden stories within everyday traditions, gaining a profound understanding of the customs that have shaped their family's journey. Each journaling entry becomes a meaningful step toward unraveling the narratives behind these enduring practices, providing a richer context to personal roots.

These prompts are an ode to the traditions that form the bedrock of family identity, urging practitioners to document the nuances, ceremonies, and rituals that have sustained their families across generations. Embracing Common Traditions encourages reflection on how these shared practices have molded personal beliefs, values, and the collective identity of a family. Through heritage journaling, individuals can celebrate the diversity of their familial inheritance, creating a timeless narrative that pays homage to the enduring significance of these common traditions.

Sharing Traditions

The exploration of specific traditions that have endured through generations adds yet another dimension to prompted heritage journaling. What customs continue to be embraced by your family? How have these traditions evolved, and what significance do they hold? Through your journal, you can not only document these traditions but also explore how they contribute to the sense of shared history and identity within your family.

Heritage Journaling Prompts

Tradition Timeline Journal: Reflect on the timeline of common traditions within your family. Journal about how these traditions have evolved, their significance, and the memories attached to each stage of their development.

Cultural Fusion Celebration: Explore how common traditions have been influenced by various cultural backgrounds within your family. Journal about the unique fusion of customs, creating a rich tapestry of shared experiences.

Tradition Reinvention Challenge: Challenge yourself to reinvent a common tradition in a creative way. Journal about the process, the reactions of family members, and the new dimensions added to the tradition through your creative reinterpretation.

Generational Tradition Exchange: Reflect on the exchange of traditions between different generations. Journal about how older generations have passed down traditions and how younger generations have contributed to their evolution.

Common Rituals Reflection: Choose a common ritual or tradition and reflect on its deeper meaning. Journal about the emotions, symbolism, and shared understanding embedded in this tradition that binds the family together.

Culinary Heritage Feast: Explore common culinary traditions within your family. Journal about the recipes, the stories behind each dish, and the sense of connection fostered through shared meals.

Festive Family Traditions Collage: Create a visual collage depicting various festive traditions within your family. Journal about the colors, textures, and shared joy represented by each tradition captured in the collage.

Generational Tradition Preservation: Reflect on the importance of preserving common traditions for future generations. Journal about the role these traditions play in maintaining a sense of continuity and unity within the family.

Common Songbook Journey: Compile a family songbook that represents common musical traditions. Journal about the stories behind each song, the memories associated with them, and their role in family gatherings.

Generational Craft Workshop: Engage in a craft workshop focused on common creative traditions within your family. Journal about the shared artistic expressions, the collaborative process, and the artifacts created during the workshop.

Seasonal Heritage Reflection: Explore how common traditions vary across different seasons within your family. Journal about the significance of these seasonal variations, the rituals involved, and the emotions they evoke.

Generational Tradition Time Capsule: Create a time capsule representing common traditions from various generations. Journal about the items included, the stories behind them, and the anticipation of future generations uncovering this cultural treasure.

The Language That Binds Generations

Heritage Journaling prompts will guide you in contemplating the unique language spoken across generations within your family. This language encompasses more than just words—it encompasses shared experiences, values, and cultural nuances. Reflect on prompts that encourage you to delve into the subtleties of this language, capturing the essence of what binds generations together.

Heritage Journaling Prompts

Family Story Exchange: Initiate a story exchange where family members share personal anecdotes. Journal about the laughter, connections, and understanding fostered through the exchange of these narratives.

Generational Perspectives Forum: Host a forum where family members from different generations discuss their perspectives on specific topics. Journal about the insights gained, encouraging a respectful and open exchange of ideas.

Ancestral Q&A Session: Facilitate a Q&A session where younger family members can ask questions to older generations. Journal about the revelations, shared wisdom, and the bond strengthened through this exchange.

Memory Lane Exploration: Explore a family photo album or memorabilia with members from various generations. Journal about the stories, laughter, and shared memories that surface, fostering a sense of connection.

Shared Hobbies Workshop: Organize a workshop where different generations can share their hobbies or skills. Journal about the diverse talents and the mutual understanding cultivated through this exchange.

Ancestral Recipe Exchange: Initiate a recipe exchange between generations. Journal about the culinary traditions shared, the memories attached to specific dishes, and the intergenerational dialogue facilitated by this activity.

Generational Interview Series: Initiate an interview series with family members from different generations. Journal about the insights gained, fostering open dialogue and understanding between the diverse age groups.

Life Lessons Letter Exchange: Encourage the exchange of letters between generations, sharing life lessons, experiences, and advice. Journal about the impact of these heartfelt letters on fostering understanding and connection.

Generational Book Club: Start a family book club that includes literature reflecting the experiences of different generations. Journal about the discussions, reflections, and insights gained through this shared reading experience.

Historical Technology Session: Create a session where younger generations share modern technology with older family members, and vice versa. Journal about the bridging of technological gaps and the exchange of knowledge between generations.

Cultural Heritage Documentary Night: Host a documentary night featuring films related to your family's cultural heritage. Journal about the discussions sparked, the shared emotions, and the deepening of connections between generations.

Generational Art Collaboration: Collaborate on an art project that involves members from different generations. Journal about the creative process, insights gained, and the bond strengthened through the shared expression of artistic talents.

Connecting across generations through Heritage Journaling is a dynamic and ongoing process. As you engage with prompts and reflect on discussions, remember that each entry contributes to the interwoven narrative of your family's history, fostering connection and understanding. The subsequent chapters of this book will continue to unravel thematic prompts, exercises, and discussions that enrich your exploration of personal and familial heritage.

Chapter 8: Celebrating Milestones and Everyday Moments

Celebrating Milestones and Everyday Moments transforms heritage journaling into a joyous commemoration of life's victories, both grand and subtle. These prompts inspire practitioners to document the extraordinary milestones and the beauty found in ordinary, everyday experiences. Each journal entry becomes a testament to the resilience of family ties and the significance of even the smallest moments. This theme encourages reflection on the role these moments play in shaping family narratives, creating a mosaic of shared joy, challenges, and the richness of everyday life.

Transmitting Values and Wisdom

Heritage Journaling serves as a vessel for the transmission of values and wisdom from one generation to the next. Delve into prompts that encourage you to explore the values held dear within your family. How are these values manifested in everyday life? Reflect on the wisdom passed down through generations and consider how these timeless teachings can be documented for posterity. Your journal becomes a repository for the invaluable lessons that shape your family's identity.

Heritage Journaling Prompts

> **Value Reflection:** Reflect on the core values that have been transmitted through generations within your family. Journal about the significance of these values, how they've shaped your identity, and the lessons learned.

Generational Wisdom Collage: Create a visual collage that represents the wisdom passed down through family members. Journal about the symbols, quotes, and images that embody the collective wisdom of your familial heritage.

Values in Action Journal: Choose a value that holds particular importance within your family. Journal about specific instances where this value was demonstrated, its impact, and how it continues to guide family decisions and actions.

Ancestral Wisdom Dialogue: Imagine a conversation with an ancestor known for their wisdom. Journal about the questions you would ask, the advice you'd seek, and the insights you'd hope to gain from this imaginary dialogue.

Ethical Dilemma Reflection: Contemplate an ethical dilemma or challenge faced by a family member in the past. Journal about the decision-making process, the values involved, and the outcomes, exploring how this scenario contributes to your family's ethical heritage.

Value-Inspired Action Plan: Select a core value and create a personalized action plan for integrating it into your daily life. Journal about the steps you plan to take, the challenges anticipated, and the positive impact you hope to achieve.

Generational Proverbs Journal: Compile a list of proverbs or sayings passed down through generations in your family. Journal about the meanings behind these proverbs, their origins, and how they encapsulate valuable life lessons.

Cultural Traditions and Values: Explore how cultural traditions within your family reflect and transmit specific values. Journal about the interplay between cultural heritage, values, and the continuity of traditions through generations.

Values in Family Rituals: Examine how family rituals are grounded in and transmit core values. Journal about specific rituals, the values they embody, and the emotional resonance they bring to family gatherings.

Generational Book of Wisdom: Create a "Book of Wisdom" where family members contribute quotes, advice, or personal mantras that embody their values. Journal about the process of compiling this collective wisdom and its significance.

Values in Parental Guidance: Reflect on the values instilled by your parents or caregivers. Journal about the lessons learned from their guidance, how these values have shaped your worldview, and the influence they continue to have in your life.

Value-Based Family Mission Statement: Collaborate with family members to create a mission statement based on shared values. Journal about the collaborative process, the values highlighted, and the sense of unity fostered by this collective vision.

Documenting Life Lessons for Posterity

In this section, prompts are designed to guide you in documenting specific life lessons that have been imparted through the ages in your family. Share stories of resilience, perseverance, and growth. Consider how these lessons have shaped family members and how they, in turn, can serve as guiding principles for future generations. Through Heritage Journaling, you contribute to the legacy of wisdom within your family.

Heritage Journaling Prompts

Life Lesson Timeline: Create a timeline of significant life lessons learned by various family members. Journal about the impact these lessons had on shaping individual paths and how they contribute to the collective family narrative.

Adversity Journal: Reflect on a challenging experience in your life or the life of a family member. Journal about the lessons extracted from overcoming adversity, the personal growth achieved, and the resilience that emerged.

Family Wisdom Quilt: Envision a metaphorical quilt made up of patches representing different life lessons from family members. Journal about the stories behind each patch, the wisdom they hold, and how this quilt symbolizes the resilience of your familial lineage.

Legacy of Resilience Reflection: Explore instances in your family history where resilience in the face of hardship was evident. Journal about the specific challenges, the resilience demonstrated, and how these stories contribute to a legacy of strength.

Turning Points Journal: Identify pivotal moments in your life or your family's history. Journal about the lessons learned during these turning points, how they redirected paths, and the wisdom gained from navigating life's twists and turns.

Life Lesson Metaphors: Choose a metaphor or symbol that represents a significant life lesson. Journal about the symbolism, the real-life context, and how this metaphorical lesson has influenced your perspectives or decisions.

Generational Lessons Dialogue: Imagine a conversation with a family member who imparted a crucial life lesson. Journal about the questions you would ask, the insights you'd seek, and how this dialogue would contribute to preserving family wisdom.

Epiphanies Journal: Record personal epiphanies or 'aha' moments in your life. Journal about the circumstances, the realizations, and the lasting impact these moments have had on your understanding of yourself and your family.

Values in Action Journal: Link specific values to life lessons experienced by family members. Journal about how these values provided guidance during challenging times, reinforcing the connection between family values and real-life application.

Narrative of Growth: Chart your personal or familial growth journey, highlighting key lessons at various stages. Journal about the evolution, the pivotal moments, and the continuous learning embedded in this ongoing narrative.

Life Lesson Letters: Write letters to future generations sharing personal life lessons and the wisdom gained. Journal about the emotions, insights, and hopes for how these letters may resonate with and guide descendants.

Narratives of Transformation: Explore stories of personal or familial transformation. Journal about the catalysts, the process of change, and the valuable lessons learned through the evolution of individuals or the family as a whole.

Passing Down Wisdom Through Stories

Wisdom often finds its way into our lives through stories—narratives that encapsulate profound insights and lessons. Craft prompts that encourage the exploration of these stories within your family. Chronicle the tales of ancestors, recount parables shared through generations, and consider how these stories serve as vessels for the passage of wisdom. Your journal becomes a narrative tapestry, interweaving the threads of collective wisdom.

Heritage Journaling Prompts

Storyteller's Circle: Create a virtual or physical circle where family members take turns sharing stories that impart wisdom. Journal about the stories exchanged, the lessons they hold, and the bond strengthened through shared narratives.

Ancestral Wisdom Chronicles: Explore ancestral wisdom by delving into the stories of older generations. Journal about the nuggets of wisdom found in ancestral tales and reflect on how these stories shape your understanding of family heritage.

Interactive Story Journal: Write an interactive story that imparts a specific piece of wisdom. Encourage family members to add their twists to the tale, creating a collaborative narrative that embodies shared family values.

Fables and Morals Exploration: Explore fables, folktales, or moral stories from your cultural background. Journal about the morals embedded in these tales and how they align with or diverge from the values upheld in your family.

Legacy of Proverbs: Collect and reflect on proverbs or sayings passed down through generations. Journal about the origins of these proverbs, their cultural significance, and the timeless wisdom encapsulated in concise phrases.

Mythical Wisdom Unveiled: Dive into myths or legends from your cultural heritage that hold inherent wisdom. Journal about the symbolic meanings, moral lessons, and the application of these myths in contemporary family life.

Family Parables Journal: Craft modern parables or allegorical stories that convey important life lessons. Journal about the inspiration behind each parable and how they can serve as instructive narratives for family members.

Personal Allegories: Transform personal experiences into allegories with underlying wisdom. Journal about the process of translating real-life events into fictional narratives that carry universal truths and lessons.

Living Legends Reflection: Identify living legends or individuals in your family who embody wisdom. Journal about the lessons learned through observing their lives, the values they personify, and the impact they've had on family dynamics.

Narrative Ethics Inquiry: Explore the ethical dimensions within family narratives. Journal about situations where family members faced moral dilemmas, the decisions made, and the lessons derived from navigating ethical challenges.

Values in Action Narratives: Document instances where family values were put into action. Journal about the alignment between stated values and actual behavior, reflecting on how these narratives contribute to the family's ethical legacy.

Cultural Wisdom Insights: Investigate cultural or traditional stories that hold profound wisdom. Journal about the cultural context, the moral teachings, and how these narratives shape your perception of what is valuable in life.

The Wisdom of Legends: Explore legendary figures or heroes within your cultural heritage. Journal about the virtues and lessons associated with these figures, considering how their stories contribute to a collective understanding of wisdom.

Heritage Journaling Through the Ages

Explore prompts that invite you to reflect on how the act of journaling has evolved through different generations within your family. How have journaling practices, methods, and purposes shifted over time? Investigate the mediums used for journaling, from handwritten diaries to digital formats. Consider how the essence of Heritage Journaling has persisted, connecting family members across ages through the shared act of documenting life.

Heritage Journaling Prompts

Ancestral Echoes Dialogue: Imagine a conversation with an ancestor from a different era. Journal about what you would ask, the insights gained, and the potential impact on your understanding of family history.

Time Capsule Chronicles: Create a digital or physical time capsule. Journal about the items or memories you would include to represent your current era and how future generations might interpret these artifacts.

Era-Infused Reflections: Pick a specific historical era significant to your family. Journal about how the events and cultural aspects of that time may have influenced your family's narrative and values.

Generational Perspectives Collage: Create a visual collage depicting snapshots from different generations of your family. Journal about the commonalities, changes, and unique aspects that define each generation.

Letters Across Time: Write a letter to a past or future family member. Journal about the emotions, advice, or insights you would share and the impact you hope it would have on the recipient.

Genealogical Timeline Mapping: Develop a visual timeline of key events and milestones in your family's history. Journal about the connections between these events and the broader historical context of each era.

Photographic Time Travel: Select a family photo from a bygone era. Journal about the people, clothing, and surroundings, imagining yourself in that moment and reflecting on the stories behind the image.

Historical Heritage Exploration: Research a historical event significant to your family's origins. Journal about how this event shaped your family's trajectory and the lasting impact on your cultural identity.

Virtual Heritage Museum: Create a virtual heritage museum showcasing artifacts or stories from different periods of your family's history. Journal about the significance of each exhibit and its role in preserving your heritage.

Narrative Evolution Inquiry: Explore how family narratives have evolved over generations. Journal about the stories that remain constant, those that have transformed, and the cultural shifts influencing these changes.

Epochal Reflections: Reflect on significant epochs in your family's history, such as migrations or major life changes. Journal about the resilience, adaptations, and shared values that threaded through these transformative periods.

Time-Traveling Traditions: Identify and explore traditions passed down through generations. Journal about the evolution of these traditions, how they adapt to contemporary times, and their role in fostering a sense of continuity.

Journaling as a Witness to Life's Milestones

Life is punctuated by significant milestones, and Heritage Journaling provides a unique vantage point to witness and commemorate these moments. Design prompts that encourage you to reflect on the major milestones within your family—births, weddings, graduations, and more. Capture the emotions, anecdotes, and reflections surrounding these events. Your journal becomes a witness to the tapestry of life's remarkable moments.

Heritage Journaling Prompts

Milestone Reflection Letters: Write letters to yourself at different life milestones. Journal about the advice, encouragement, and reflections you would share with your past and future selves.

Life's Crossroads Exploration: Reflect on pivotal moments where life took unexpected turns. Journal about the emotions, decisions made, and the impact of these crossroads on your personal and family narrative.

The Journal of Firsts: Create a dedicated journal for documenting significant firsts—first job, home, love. Journal about the emotions experienced during these milestones and their lasting effects.

Rite of Passage Reflections: Explore cultural or personal rites of passage. Journal about the symbolism, lessons, and transformations associated with these milestones in your life.

Legacy-Building Milestones: Reflect on milestones that contribute to your legacy. Journal about the intentional actions and achievements that shape the narrative you're building for future generations.

Cross-Generational Celebrations: Journal about celebrations that have transcended generations in your family. Reflect on the evolution of these festivities and the shared joy across different age groups.

Life Chapters Journaling: Divide your life into distinct chapters. Journal about the defining moments, challenges, and growth experienced in each chapter, creating a comprehensive autobiography over time.

Reflections on Turning Points: Explore turning points in your life. Journal about the lessons learned, the people who influenced these shifts, and how these pivotal moments shaped your character.

Shared Life Journeys: Connect with family members to explore shared milestones. Journal about the collective memories, shared joys, and challenges that weave together to form a rich tapestry of familial experiences.

Growth and Transformation Diary: Create a diary tracking personal growth over the years. Journal about the transformative moments, mindset shifts, and the continuous evolution of your identity.

Milestone Manifesto: Develop a personal manifesto for approaching life milestones. Journal about the values, intentions, and guiding principles you wish to uphold during significant moments.

Reflections on Legacy Milestones: Reflect on the milestones you aspire to leave as part of your legacy. Journal about the intentional steps taken to build a meaningful and enduring impact on future generations.

Commemorating Everyday Victories and Challenges

Beyond grand milestones, everyday life is replete with victories and challenges. Explore prompts that prompt you to document the smaller triumphs and struggles that collectively shape your family's journey. Reflect on the resilience demonstrated in the face of challenges and celebrate the victories, no matter how modest. Heritage Journaling captures the nuanced rhythm of daily life, providing a holistic view of your family's collective experiences.

Heritage Journaling Prompts

Daily Triumphs Journal: Create a daily journal focusing on small victories. Journal about the triumphs, no matter how minor, and the positive impact they have on your overall well-being.

Challenge Reflection Letters: Write letters to yourself during challenging times. Journal about the coping mechanisms, resilience, and lessons learned during periods of adversity.

Family Resilience Diary: Collaborate with family members to document collective resilience. Journal about how the family has overcome challenges together and the strength drawn from shared experiences.

Daily Gratitude Log: Establish a gratitude log for daily reflections. Journal about the small moments of gratitude, creating a chronicle of positivity even during challenging times.

Adversity to Strength Stories: Explore family stories of overcoming adversity. Journal about the strength, courage, and lessons embedded in these narratives, emphasizing the collective resilience of your family.

Celebrating Persistence Journal: Create a dedicated journal to celebrate persistence and perseverance. Journal about the challenges faced, the steps taken to overcome them, and the growth achieved through persistence.

Everyday Heroes Exploration: Identify everyday heroes within your family. Journal about the challenges they've conquered and the lessons their stories offer, emphasizing the unsung triumphs within the family.

Shared Challenges Diary: Collaborate with family members to document shared challenges. Journal about the strategies employed, the mutual support, and the sense of unity cultivated during difficult times.

Victories in the Mundane: Reflect on everyday victories often overlooked. Journal about the beauty found in ordinary moments, emphasizing how these small wins contribute to the overall family narrative.

Trial and Triumph Dialogue: Write a dialogue between yourself during challenging times and your present self. Journal about the growth, insights, and resilience gained through navigating difficulties.

Strength in Diversity Journal: Explore how different family members approach and overcome challenges. Journal about the diversity of perspectives, coping mechanisms, and the collective strength derived from this diversity.

Daily Affirmations for Resilience: Develop daily affirmations focused on resilience. Journal about the impact of affirmations on mindset during challenging moments, creating a resource for cultivating resilience.

Fostering a Shared Identity

Prompt exploration in this section encourages you to consider how the act of celebrating milestones and everyday moments contributes to fostering a shared identity within your family. What rituals, traditions, or commemorations serve as touchpoints for identity formation? How do these shared experiences contribute to a sense of belonging and unity? Your journal becomes a canvas for illustrating the collective identity woven through the fabric of family life.

Heritage Journaling Prompts

Family Crest Exploration: Journal about your family's crest or symbols that represent your shared identity. Reflect on the elements that make up this emblem and explore the stories and values it encapsulates.

Origin Story Unveiling: Dive into the origins of your family's surname or name. Journal about the discoveries, surprises, or historical insights that contribute to shaping your family's shared identity.

Roots Journey Mapping: Create a map tracing the geographical roots of your family. Journal about the places significant to your shared identity and the emotional connections these locations hold for your family.

Coat of Arms Interpretation: Explore the meaning behind your family's coat of arms. Journal about the colors, animals, or symbols used and how they align with the shared identity and values of your family lineage.

Shared Ancestral Talents: Reflect on and journal about any shared talents or skills that have been passed down through generations within your family. Explore how these talents contribute to your shared identity.

Family Motto Reflection: If your family has a motto, explore its origins and meaning. Journal about how this motto encapsulates the principles and beliefs that form the foundation of your shared identity.

Cultural Heritage Showcase: Dedicate a journal entry to showcasing elements of your family's cultural heritage. Explore traditions, customs, or artifacts that contribute to your shared identity, fostering a sense of pride and connection.

Historical Family Achievements: Reflect on and journal about notable achievements or milestones in your family's history. Explore how these accomplishments contribute to your shared identity and the values they represent.

Ancestral Stories Collage: Create a visual or written collage of ancestral stories. Journal about the diverse narratives that contribute to your family's shared identity, fostering a deeper understanding of your roots.

Emblem of Unity: If your family has a symbol or emblem that represents unity, journal about its significance. Reflect on how this emblem fosters a sense of togetherness and shared identity among family members.

Historical Family Resilience: Explore instances of resilience and strength within your family's history. Journal about how overcoming challenges has shaped your shared identity, fostering a sense of fortitude.

Intergenerational Values Tree: Create a metaphorical tree depicting the values passed down through generations. Journal about the roots (ancestors), trunk (shared values), and branches (individual family members) that contribute to your shared identity.

Creating a Legacy Through Shared Experiences

Legacy is built not only on monumental events but also on the accumulation of shared experiences. Utilize prompts to reflect on how everyday moments contribute to the creation of a lasting legacy within your family. Consider how seemingly ordinary occurrences, when documented, become threads in the rich tapestry of family history. Heritage Journaling transforms the mundane into the extraordinary, ensuring that each shared experience is valued and preserved.

Heritage Journaling Prompts

Legacy-Building Adventures: Plan and undertake an adventure or project with family members. Journal about the experiences, challenges, and the lasting memories created as part of building a shared legacy.

Collaborative Memory-Making Journal: Create a shared journal for collaborative memory-making. Journal about the collective experiences documented by family members, emphasizing the importance of shared stories in building a legacy.

Shared Artistic Endeavors: Explore artistic endeavors as a family. Journal about collaborative projects, such as creating family art, music, or literature, that contribute to a lasting artistic legacy.

Time Capsule Creation: As a family, create a time capsule capturing the essence of your current moment. Journal about the items chosen, the significance behind them, and the anticipation of future generations opening the capsule.

Digital Legacy Collage: Develop a digital collage showcasing significant moments and achievements. Journal about the digital artifacts chosen and their representation of a shared legacy in the age of technology.

Legacy-Building Traditions: Establish traditions focused on building a legacy. Journal about the intentional steps taken, such as family reunions, storytelling sessions, or collaborative projects, to contribute to the family's lasting impact.

Narrative Heirloom Reflections: Identify narrative heirlooms within your family. Journal about the stories, anecdotes, and personal artifacts passed down through generations, highlighting their role in building a shared legacy.

Family Values Manifesto: Collaborate with family members to create a values manifesto. Journal about the core values identified, the discussions held, and the collective commitment to upholding these values as part of the family legacy.

Shared Philanthropic Endeavors: Engage in philanthropic endeavors as a family. Journal about the impact of collective giving, the causes supported, and the legacy of compassion and social responsibility fostered within the family.

Culinary Legacy Chronicles: Chronicle the culinary legacy of your family. Journal about traditional recipes, the stories behind them, and the role of food in shaping a distinct family identity that is passed down through generations.

Interconnected Achievements Journal: Reflect on interconnected achievements within the family. Journal about the milestones reached collectively and the sense of pride and legacy associated with these shared accomplishments.

Educational Legacy Exploration: Explore the educational legacy within your family. Journal about shared educational values, stories of academic achievements, and the importance placed on learning as part of the family's legacy.

The Role of Everyday Moments in Family History

Delve into prompts that prompt you to contemplate the significance of everyday moments in the larger narrative of family history. How do routine activities, daily interactions, and shared rituals contribute to the overarching story? Reflect on the role these moments play in shaping familial bonds and cultural practices. Through your journal, you recognize the profound impact of the seemingly ordinary, enriching the tapestry of family history.

Heritage Journaling Prompts

Everyday Ritual Reflections: Reflect on daily rituals and routines within the family. Journal about the significance of these everyday moments and their role in shaping the family narrative.

Snapshot Chronicles: Create a journal dedicated to snapshots of everyday life. Journal about the ordinary yet meaningful moments captured in photos, showcasing the beauty found in everyday family life.

Communal Meals Journal: Chronicle communal meals shared as a family. Journal about the conversations, laughter, and connections forged during these everyday rituals that contribute to the family narrative.

Seasonal Traditions Diary: Document seasonal traditions observed within your family. Journal about the unique celebrations, rituals, and stories associated with each season, creating a comprehensive account of yearly traditions.

Everyday Wisdom Repository: Create a repository for everyday wisdom shared within the family. Journal about the lessons, advice, and insights gained from everyday conversations that contribute to the family's collective wisdom.

Spontaneous Adventure Journal: Dedicate a journal to spontaneous adventures. Journal about unplanned trips, surprises, and serendipitous moments that add spontaneity and excitement to the family narrative.

Growth Through Everyday Challenges: Reflect on the growth achieved through everyday challenges. Journal about overcoming obstacles, adapting to change, and the resilience cultivated during the ebb and flow of everyday life.

Homemade Traditions Exploration: Explore homemade traditions within your family. Journal about the rituals, games, or activities created by family members that have become cherished and integral aspects of everyday life.

Technology in Everyday Moments: Explore the role of technology in capturing everyday moments. Journal about the ways in which digital tools contribute to documenting and preserving the family narrative.

Bedtime Story Chronicles: Chronicle bedtime stories shared within the family. Journal about the tales told, the lessons conveyed, and the bonding experiences created through these everyday storytelling moments.

Everyday Connections Journal: Reflect on connections formed through everyday interactions. Journal about the relationships, laughter, and shared experiences that contribute to the fabric of family connections.

Family Meeting Notes: Keep notes from family meetings. Journal about the discussions held, decisions made, and the collaborative efforts that shape the everyday governance of family life.

Celebrating Milestones and Everyday Moments through Heritage Journaling allows you to capture the essence of life's journey in its entirety. Each prompt and reflection contributes to the creation of a family narrative that honors both the extraordinary and the everyday. As you engage with these themes, you are not just documenting events; you are weaving a narrative that resonates across generations, celebrating the unique journey of your family.

"Family is not an important thing, it's everything."

Michael J. Fox

Chapter 9: Final Reflections and Encouragement

Final Reflections and Encouragement mark the poignant culmination of the heritage journaling journey. These prompts invite practitioners to reflect on the transformative power of their narratives, acknowledging the beauty found in the imperfections of the journaling process. It serves as a gentle nudge to embrace unfiltered, authentic storytelling. The theme encourages individuals to celebrate the uniqueness of their journey, finding solace and empowerment in the imperfections. As heritage journaling becomes a tool for self-discovery, these prompts offer words of encouragement, inspiring practitioners to revel in the beauty of their distinctive and evolving family narratives.

The Impact of Heritage Journaling

As you embark on the concluding chapter of your Heritage Journaling journey, take a moment to reflect on the profound impact this practice has had on your understanding of personal and family history. Explore prompts that guide you in articulating the shifts in your perspective, the newfound insights, and the connections you've forged through the act of journaling. Your journal serves as a testament to the transformative power of Heritage Journaling in shaping your genealogical journey.

Heritage Journaling Prompts

Reflect on Your Journey: Take a moment to reflect on your heritage journaling journey so far. Journal about the impact it has had on your understanding of family history, cultural identity, and personal growth.

Shared Insights: Collaborate with a family member to journal about the shared insights gained through heritage journaling. Explore common themes, differences in perspectives, and the collective impact on family narratives.

Unearthed Treasures: Journal about any unexpected discoveries or hidden family treasures that heritage journaling has unearthed. Capture the joy and significance of stumbling upon valuable pieces of your family's history.

Connecting the Dots: Explore how heritage journaling has helped you connect the dots between generations. Journal about the bridges built, the gaps filled, and the sense of continuity fostered through documenting your family's heritage.

Deepened Cultural Understanding: Reflect on how heritage journaling has deepened your understanding of cultural practices within your family. Journal about the traditions, rituals, and customs that have come to life through the process.

Impact on Relationships: Journal about the impact of heritage journaling on your relationships with family members. Explore how shared stories and reflections have strengthened bonds, creating a deeper sense of connection.

Preserving Family Stories: Document the impact of heritage journaling on preserving family stories. Journal about the satisfaction of contributing to the longevity of your family's narrative and the importance of passing down these stories.

Cultural Legacy for Future Generations: Consider the legacy heritage journaling will leave for future generations. Journal about the responsibility and privilege of contributing to a cultural legacy that will be cherished by those who come after you.

Evolving Perspectives: Explore how your perspectives on family history and heritage have evolved through journaling. Journal about the shifts in perception, newfound appreciations, and a deeper connection to your roots.

Bridge to Ancestral Roots: Reflect on heritage journaling as a bridge to your ancestral roots. Journal about the sense of continuity, belonging, and the spiritual connection forged by exploring and documenting your heritage.

Celebrating Diversity: Journal about how heritage journaling has enabled you to celebrate the diversity within your family. Explore the richness derived from embracing different cultural influences and stories.

Community Impact: Consider the broader impact of heritage journaling within your community. Journal about the potential for shared stories to foster a sense of community and cultural pride among those connected by similar histories.

Transformative Experiences

Document prompts that guide you in recounting and reflecting upon the transformative moments you've experienced throughout your Heritage Journaling journey. Share anecdotes of discoveries that deepened your understanding of your cultural roots, revelations that bridged generational gaps, and the emotional landscapes traversed in the pursuit of family history. Your journal becomes a treasure trove of personal metamorphoses and milestones.

Heritage Journaling Prompts

Personal Growth Journey: Document your personal growth journey through heritage journaling. Journal about the transformative experiences, lessons learned, and the evolution of your mindset and self-awareness.

Navigating Challenges: Reflect on how heritage journaling has helped you navigate challenges. Journal about the resilience cultivated, coping mechanisms discovered, and the transformative power of storytelling in overcoming adversity.

Discovery of Resilience: Journal about the moments of resilience discovered through heritage journaling. Explore the stories of ancestors who exhibited strength in challenging times and draw inspiration for your own journey.

Mindfulness and Reflection: Explore how heritage journaling has introduced mindfulness and reflection into your life. Journal about the meditative qualities of the process and the transformative impact on your overall well-being.

Cultural Connection as Healing: Journal about the healing power of connecting with your cultural roots. Explore how heritage journaling has been a transformative experience in fostering a sense of belonging, pride, and healing.

Embracing Complexity: Reflect on the transformative experience of embracing the complexity within your family's history. Journal about navigating nuanced narratives, challenging assumptions, and growing through the acceptance of imperfections.

Family Unity and Transformation: Document instances where heritage journaling has contributed to family unity and transformation. Journal about shared experiences, collective growth, and the strength derived from embracing the family's collective narrative.

Legacy of Transformation: Consider the legacy of transformation you aspire to leave through heritage journaling. Journal about the values, stories, and lessons you aim to pass down as a testament to the transformative power of preserving family history.

Discovering Hidden Talents: Reflect on any hidden talents or creative expressions discovered through heritage journaling. Journal about the transformative experience of unlocking new aspects of yourself during the exploration of family history.

Self-Discovery Through Ancestry: Explore how heritage journaling has been a tool for self-discovery through understanding your ancestry. Journal about the transformative moments when ancestral stories shed light on your own identity and purpose.

Shaping Future Narratives: Journal about the transformative role of heritage journaling in shaping future narratives. Reflect on how the practice lays the foundation for future generations, providing a roadmap for continued exploration, understanding, and celebration of cultural heritage.

Embracing Imperfections

Explore prompts that embrace the imperfections inherent in the journaling process. Reflect on moments of vulnerability, the beauty found in unfiltered narratives, and the authenticity that emerges when imperfections are acknowledged. Your journal is not just a record of facts; it's a testament to the imperfect, yet beautifully authentic, nature of your genealogical exploration. Embrace the imperfections, for they add depth and character to your family narrative.

Heritage Journaling Prompts

Journaling Without Judgment: Embrace the imperfections in the journaling process by practicing nonjudgmental observation. Journal about the freedom and self-compassion that come from allowing your thoughts and expressions to flow without harsh self-criticism.

Authenticity Over Perfection: Reflect on the value of authenticity over perfection in heritage journaling. Journal about the beauty and depth that arise when embracing the authenticity of your voice, even if it means letting go of the pursuit of perfection.

Celebrating Unfiltered Thoughts: Embrace unfiltered thoughts and expressions in your heritage journal. Journal about the liberation that comes from allowing raw, unpolished ideas to take shape on paper, capturing the genuine essence of your reflections.

Navigating Uncertainty: Explore the imperfections in navigating uncertainty within the journaling process. Journal about how the unknown, the unresolved, and the ambiguous aspects of your family history can be embraced as part of the evolving narrative.

The Beauty of Unscripted Stories: Reflect on the beauty of unscripted stories within your heritage journal. Journal about the charm and authenticity that arise when stories unfold naturally, unburdened by rigid structures or predefined narratives.

Embracing Mistakes as Learning: Embrace mistakes as valuable learning experiences in heritage journaling. Journal about how missteps, errors, and detours can lead to unexpected insights, growth, and a more resilient approach to storytelling.

Unearthing Hidden Imperfections: Reflect on the process of unearthing hidden imperfections in family history. Journal about the stories, quirks, and idiosyncrasies that add depth and character to your family's narrative, even if they deviate from societal ideals.

Journey of Self-Discovery: Embrace the imperfections as part of the journey of self-discovery. Journal about the self-awareness and personal insights that emerge when you allow imperfections to coexist with the genuine exploration of your family's heritage.

Artistic Freedom in Expression: Reflect on the artistic freedom in expression within heritage journaling. Journal about the joy and creativity that come from liberating your expressions, allowing your unique style and voice to shine through.

Unpolished Beauty of Stories: Embrace the unpolished beauty of stories within your family history. Journal about the charm and allure of narratives that may not conform to conventional storytelling standards but resonate with authenticity.

Mindful Acceptance of Flaws: Practice mindful acceptance of flaws in the journaling process. Journal about cultivating a sense of peace and self-compassion by acknowledging and embracing the imperfections inherent in the storytelling journey.

Appreciating Unfinished Tales: Reflect on the appreciation of unfinished tales within your heritage journal. Journal about the beauty found in narratives that are still evolving, recognizing that the process of storytelling is ongoing and never truly complete.

The Beauty of Unfiltered Journaling

Dive into prompts that encourage unfiltered, raw expressions within your journal. Reflect on the moments when you allowed your thoughts and emotions to flow freely onto the pages. Celebrate the unedited, unpolished beauty of your journal entries. Your journal becomes a canvas where the authenticity of your voice is preserved—a testament to the unfiltered essence of your genealogical exploration.

Heritage Journaling Prompts

Raw Emotions on Paper: Explore the beauty of expressing raw emotions on paper in your heritage journal. Journal about the authenticity and power that come from allowing genuine feelings, whether joyous or challenging, to be articulated unfiltered.

Spontaneous Storytelling: Embrace spontaneous storytelling in your heritage journal. Journal about the joy and freedom of allowing narratives to unfold naturally, without overthinking or scripting, capturing the unfiltered essence of your family's history.

Unfiltered Creativity Release: Reflect on the release of unfiltered creativity within heritage journaling. Journal about the moments of inspiration, innovation, and imaginative expression that arise when you give yourself the freedom to create without constraints.

Free-Flowing Narrative Threads: Explore the beauty of free-flowing narrative threads within your family history. Journal about the interconnected stories, diverse perspectives, and meandering paths that contribute to the rich tapestry of your family's collective narrative.

Capturing Authentic Moments: Capture authentic moments through unfiltered journaling. Journal about the unscripted events, everyday interactions, and candid experiences that bring life to your family's story, allowing for a genuine representation of the moments that matter.

Celebrating Unedited Insights: Celebrate unedited insights within your heritage journal. Journal about the revelations, epiphanies, and unfiltered observations that emerge when you refrain from self-editing, allowing your thoughts to unfold organically.

Real-Time Reflections: Reflect on the beauty of real-time reflections in your heritage journal. Journal about the immediacy and sincerity that come from recording thoughts and experiences as they happen, preserving the unfiltered essence of the moment.

Authentic Dialogue Capture: Embrace the authentic capture of dialogue within heritage journaling. Journal about the power of transcribing conversations, preserving the unique voices and expressions of family members, and capturing the unfiltered nature of interpersonal communication.

Uninhibited Creative Expression: Explore uninhibited creative expression in your heritage journal. Journal about the joy and fulfillment found in experimenting with various forms of expression, whether through drawings, poems, or other creative outlets, without the constraints of perfection.

Emotional Release on the Page: Journal about the emotional release that comes from laying bare your feelings on the page. Explore the therapeutic and cathartic aspects of unfiltered journaling, allowing the page to become a safe space for emotional expression.

Vivid Snapshot Narratives: Embrace vivid snapshot narratives within your heritage journal. Journal about the beauty of capturing specific moments, memories, or anecdotes in their raw and unfiltered form, creating a collection of vibrant and authentic snapshots.

Freedom in Narrative Evolution: Reflect on the freedom found in the evolution of narratives within heritage journaling. Journal about how allowing stories to evolve organically, free from predefined structures, contributes to the dynamic and ever-unfolding nature of your family's history.

Encouragement to Celebrate the Unique Journey

Conclude your Heritage Journaling journey with prompts that inspire you to celebrate the uniqueness of your genealogical exploration. Reflect on the distinctive twists and turns, the unexpected discoveries, and the personal revelations that have shaped your journey. Your journal becomes a tribute to the singular path you've navigated, honoring the nuances that make your family history journey truly one-of-a-kind.

Heritage Journaling Prompts

Honoring Personal Progress: Encourage yourself to celebrate personal progress in your heritage journal. Journal about the steps you've taken, the growth you've experienced, and the evolving nature of your journey through the lens of family history.

Acknowledging Resilience: Acknowledge your resilience in the face of challenges within heritage journaling. Journal about the hurdles you've overcome, the lessons learned, and the strength you've gained throughout your exploration of family narratives.

Embracing Diverse Narratives: Embrace the diversity of narratives within your family history. Journal about the unique perspectives, varied experiences, and distinct voices that contribute to the richness of your heritage, encouraging the celebration of diversity.

Finding Joy in the Process: Encourage the discovery of joy in the process of heritage journaling. Journal about the moments of happiness, inspiration, and fulfillment that arise when engaging with family stories, reinforcing the idea that the journey itself is a source of joy.

Expressing Gratitude for Insights: Express gratitude for the insights gained through heritage journaling. Journal about the valuable lessons, newfound understandings, and meaningful connections that have emerged, fostering a sense of appreciation for the richness of your family's narrative.

Embracing Family Complexity: Encourage the embrace of family complexity within your heritage journal. Journal about the beauty found in the multifaceted nature of family relationships, understanding that the intricate tapestry of your family's story is a testament to its depth and complexity.

Recognizing the Power of Your Voice: Recognize the power of your voice in heritage journaling. Journal about the unique perspective, individuality, and authenticity that your voice brings to the storytelling process, celebrating the role you play in shaping the narrative.

Honoring Ancestral Legacy: Honor the legacy of your ancestors by acknowledging their impact on your heritage journaling journey. Journal about the wisdom, resilience, and cultural contributions passed down through generations, recognizing their enduring influence on your narrative.

Embracing Imperfections as Character: Embrace imperfections as character within heritage journaling. Journal about the quirks, idiosyncrasies, and unique qualities that add character and depth to your family's story, acknowledging that perfection is not a prerequisite for a meaningful narrative.

Cultivating a Positive Perspective: Cultivate a positive perspective on your heritage journaling journey. Journal about the moments of positivity, optimism, and hope that arise from engaging with family history, reinforcing the idea that every step forward is a cause for celebration.

Creating Space for Creative Expression: Encourage the creation of space for creative expression in your heritage journal. Journal about the liberating and empowering experience of expressing yourself creatively, whether through writing, art, or other forms, celebrating the diversity of creative outlets.

Valuing Your Contribution: Value your contribution to the family narrative through heritage journaling. Journal about the significance of your role in preserving, interpreting, and adding to the collective story, recognizing that your unique perspective enriches the overall tapestry of your family's history.

As you pen the final reflections in your Heritage Journal, remember that this is not just an endpoint but a continuation of your journey into the vast tapestry of cultural heritage and family history. Your journal is a living document, evolving as you delve deeper into your roots and create a legacy for future generations.

May your Heritage Journaling journey be a source of inspiration, connection, and celebration—a timeless record of the rich narrative that is your family history.

Appendix

Inspirational Quotes

Additional Family Heritage Prompts

Inspirational Quotes

On Family Heritage and History

"Our roots may be different, but our family tree is the same."

"In every conceivable manner, the family is a link to our past, bridge to our future." - Alex Haley

"Family is not an important thing. It's everything." - Michael J. Fox

"Heritage is not just something inherited from the past; it is also something to be passed on to the future."

"Family is the compass that guides us; a place where we feel understood and loved." - Brad Henry

"The love of family and the admiration of friends are much more important than wealth and privilege." - Charles Kuralt

"Our ancestors planted the trees; we enjoy the shade."

"Family is the fabric of life; it ties us together through thick and thin."

"A family is a place where minds come in contact with one another." - Buddha

"Our family heritage is the tapestry of our stories, woven with threads of love, laughter, and shared experiences."

"Family is the key to unlocking the door to a legacy that lives on through generations."

"The heritage of a family is not just about the names on a family tree; it's about the stories in its branches."

"Family: where life begins and love never ends."

"Our family is a circle of strength and love; every crisis faced together makes the circle stronger." - Harriet Morgan

"Roots to guide us, wings to inspire us – family is both our foundation and our aspiration."

"A family's heritage is a living legacy, passed down through the ages with the wisdom of our ancestors."

"Family heritage is a treasure chest of memories, wisdom, and love."

"Our family history is like a book, and each generation writes a new chapter."

"In the garden of family life, the love we plant is the most precious flower."

"Preserving our family heritage is not just about the past; it's an investment in the future."

"Families are the compasses that guide us; they are the inspiration to reach great heights and our comfort when we occasionally falter." - Brad Henry

"Our heritage is the sum total of all those who have gone before, whispering the lessons of their lives into our hearts."

"A family legacy is not just what we inherit; it's also about what we pass on."

"The story of a family is like a quilt. Each piece is unique, stitched with care, and when woven together, it creates a warm, comforting masterpiece."

"Our family heritage is a book written by many hands, each chapter adding to the richness of the narrative."

"Family: the echo of laughter, the shadow of memories, and the beacon of love that never fades."

"A family's heritage is the bridge between the past and the future, connecting generations with the wisdom of time."

"In the heart of every family lies a story that deserves to be told, retold, and cherished."

"Family is the thread that weaves the fabric of our lives; heritage is the tapestry that binds us together."

"Our heritage is not just a legacy; it's a gift, a treasure trove of experiences, values, and shared love."

"Family is the foundation upon which we build our dreams, and heritage is the compass that guides us on the journey."

"The branches of our family tree may stretch far and wide, but the roots run deep with the strength of generations."

"A family's heritage is like a timeless melody; it resonates across time, echoing the harmonies of love and tradition."

"In the book of life, family heritage is the most cherished chapter, written with the ink of love and memories."

"Our heritage is the symphony of voices that have shaped our story, a beautiful composition passed down from generation to generation."

"Family heritage is the soul's footprint left behind, imprinting the sands of time with the essence of who we are."

"A family's heritage is the quilt of identity, stitched together with the threads of shared values, traditions, and love."

"In the mosaic of life, family heritage adds the colors that make our story vibrant, diverse, and uniquely ours."

"Family heritage is the compass that points us towards our roots while allowing us to spread our wings and embrace the future."

"Our family heritage is a living legacy, a testament to resilience, love, and the enduring spirit of those who came before us."

On Writing

"Start writing, no matter what. The water does not flow until the faucet is turned on." - Louis L'Amour

"You can always edit a bad page. You can't edit a blank page." - Jodi Picoult

"The scariest moment is always just before you start." - Stephen King

"Don't be a writer; be writing." - William Faulkner

"Write what should not be forgotten." - Isabel Allende

"The only way to do great work is to love what you do." - Steve Jobs

"Every writer I know has trouble writing." - Joseph Heller

"The first draft is just you telling yourself the story." - Terry Pratchett

"You fail only if you stop writing." - Ray Bradbury

"The desire to write grows with writing." - Desiderius Erasmus

"You are a writer when you tell yourself you are." - F. Scott Fitzgerald

"Start writing, keep writing, and don't stop writing no matter what." - Michael Connelly

"The art of writing is the art of discovering what you believe." - Gustave Flaubert

"Your intuition knows what to write, so get out of the way." - Ray Bradbury

"The beautiful part of writing is that you don't have to get it right the first time; unlike, say, a brain surgeon." - Robert Cormier

"The more you write, the more you develop a unique voice." - David Levithan

"The best way to predict the future is to create it." - Peter Drucker

"The worst enemy to creativity is self-doubt." - Sylvia Plath

"You can make anything by writing." - C.S. Lewis

"Don't watch the clock; do what it does. Keep going." - Sam Levenson

"Writing is an exploration. You start from nothing, and learn as you go." - E.L. Doctorow

"There is no greater agony than bearing an untold story inside you." - Maya Angelou

"The only rule is to write something worth reading." - Benjamin Franklin

"A professional writer is an amateur who didn't quit." - Richard Bach

"Don't write to become famous or to make a lot of money. Write because you love it." - J.K. Rowling

"Writing is the painting of the voice." - Voltaire

"You have to write the book that wants to be written. And if the book will be too difficult for grown-ups, then you write it for children." - Madeleine L'Engle

"The hardest part is believing in yourself at the notebook stage. It is like believing in dreams in the morning." - Erica Jong

"You write to communicate to the hearts and minds of others what's burning inside you. And we edit to let the fire show through the smoke." - Arthur Plotnik

"Writing is a way of talking without being interrupted." - Jules Renard

"Writing is like driving at night in the fog. You can only see as far as your headlights, but you can make the whole trip that way." - E.L. Doctorow

"The role of a writer is not to say what we all can say, but what we are unable to say." - Anaïs Nin

"Writing is not just putting words on a page; it's discovering the world inside your head." - Stephanie Lennox

"Your writing voice is the deepest possible reflection of who you are. The job of your voice is not to seduce or flatter or make well-shaped sentences. In your voice, your readers should be able to hear the contents of your mind, your heart, your soul." - Meg Rosoff

"If there's a book that you want to read, but it hasn't been written yet, then you must write it." - Toni Morrison

"To produce a mighty book, you must choose a mighty theme." - Herman Melville

"Don't let anyone define what you write. Write the stories that you want to read." - Sherrilyn Kenyon

"The beautiful part of writing is that you don't have to get it right the first time; unlike, say, a brain surgeon." - Robert Cormier

"Write with the door closed, rewrite with the door open." - Stephen King

"Writers write. Everyone else makes excuses." - Chuck Wendig

Affirmations for Writers

"My creativity flows effortlessly, and my words have the power to inspire and resonate."

"I am a vessel of unique stories, and my writing voice is a gift to the world."

"With every word I write, I am creating a tapestry of imagination and emotion."

"I embrace the process of writing, finding joy in every sentence and paragraph."

"My mind is a wellspring of ideas, and I trust in my ability to bring them to life."

"Each word I type is a step closer to realizing my full potential as a writer."

"I release self-doubt and welcome the confidence that fuels my creative expression."

"Every setback is a setup for a comeback; I persist in my writing journey with resilience."

"I honor my unique perspective, knowing that my voice is essential in the literary landscape."

"My creativity knows no bounds; I am a boundless source of inspiration for myself and others."

"I write with intention, infusing my words with passion, purpose, and authenticity."

"My writing journey is a marathon, not a sprint, and I celebrate each step forward."

"I am a magnet for opportunities that align with my writing goals and aspirations."

"I am open to the flow of ideas, and I trust that the right words will come to me effortlessly."

"My writing space is sacred, and within it, I find the focus and clarity to bring my ideas to fruition."

"I am a constant learner, evolving with each word written and each story told."

"I release the need for perfection and embrace the beauty of my imperfect, evolving craft."

"My imagination is a boundless playground, and I joyfully explore its depths in my writing."

"I attract a supportive writing community that uplifts, inspires, and celebrates my successes."

"With each word, I am weaving a legacy of creativity, leaving an indelible mark on the literary world."

"My writing journey is a reflection of growth, resilience, and the continuous pursuit of excellence."

"I trust in the ebb and flow of my creative energy, allowing inspiration to come naturally."

"Every word I write contributes to the rich tapestry of my authorial identity."

"I am a writer with purpose, and my words have the power to spark change and understanding."

"I am an author in the making, embracing the journey as much as the destination."

"My writing is a reflection of my authentic self, and I celebrate the uniqueness I bring to the literary world."

"In the silence of my writing space, I find the strength and focus to craft stories that resonate."

"I am a conduit for creativity, channeling ideas into narratives that captivate and inspire."

"I release any fear of judgment and trust that my writing is a valuable contribution to the world."

"With each revision, my writing becomes more polished and refined, revealing the true essence of my voice."

"I am attuned to the symphony of words within me, composing stories that linger in the hearts of readers."

"My writer's block is a temporary pause, and I am always one idea away from a creative breakthrough."

"My commitment to daily writing practices strengthens my skills and hones my storytelling abilities."

"I attract literary agents, publishers, and opportunities that align with my writing goals."

"I am resilient in the face of rejection, using feedback as a stepping stone to improvement."

"My writing process is a dynamic dance of creativity, discipline, and inspiration."

"I am a master storyteller, capable of crafting narratives that transport readers to new worlds."

"I infuse my writing with passion, injecting life into characters, plots, and settings."

"I trust the timing of my writing journey, knowing that each phase serves a purpose in my growth."

"My words have the power to create connections, fostering a sense of understanding and empathy among readers."

Printed in Great Britain
by Amazon